Not Just a Babysitter

Other Redleaf Guides for Parents

- *Behavior Matters*

Not Just a Babysitter
Making Child Care Work for You

Julie Powers
with Yvonne Pearson

Redleaf Press
St. Paul, Minnesota
www.redleafpress.org

Published by Redleaf Press
a division of Resources for Child Caring
10 Yorkton Court
St. Paul, MN 55117
Visit us online at www.redleafpress.org.

© 2005 Redleaf Press
Cover design by Lightbourne
Cover illustration by Patrice Barton
Typeset in Adobe Caslon

Redleaf Press books are available at a special discount when purchased in bulk for special premiums and sales promotions. For details, contact the sales manager at 800-423-8309.

Library of Congress Cataloging-in-Publication Data
Powers, Julie, 1957-
  Not just a babysitter : making child care work for you / Julie Powers
with Yvonne Pearson.
     p. cm. -- (Redleaf guides for parents)
  ISBN-10: 1-929610-75-0
  ISBN-13: 978-1-929610-75-4
 1. Child care. 2. Child care services. 3. Parents--Services for. I.
Pearson, Yvonne. II. Title. III. Series.
  HQ778.5.P69 2005
  362.71'2--dc22
                                        2005015961

Manufactured in the United States of America
12 11 10 09 08 07 06 05   1 2 3 4 5 6 7 8

Printed on acid-free paper.

Not Just a Babysitter

Child Development Issues

A Good Fit

Foreword

Making Child Care Work for You

You are among the more than half of working parents in the United States who have made the momentous decision to put their young children into child care. Whether you have chosen a private center, a school-based program, or a family child care provider, you want this to be a place where your child will be nurtured, safe, and provided with challenging, developmentally appropriate learning experiences.

Reading this book places you among those parents who want to take an ongoing active role in ensuring that their child has a quality child care experience. Advancing quality child care has been the mission of Redleaf Press and its parent nonprofit organization, Resources for Child Caring, for over thirty years. When women began entering the workforce in record numbers in the 1970s, Resources for Child Caring was one of the first organizations in the country to help parents find child care and advocate for quality child care for all children. We know children, child care, early education, and what parents value. As a leading publisher of educational materials for child care professionals, Redleaf Press has brought together its knowledge and resources—including authors who are nationally recognized experts in the field—to create the Redleaf Guides for Parents series.

This series offers practical, easy-to-implement suggestions for enriching your child's experience in child care. Early childhood experts have identified the quality of that experience as an important ingredient in preparing your child for school. Recent brain research has revealed how critical the first five years are to a child's development. During these years the brain grows at its fastest rate, and connections between neurons in the brain are made rapidly. It is these connections that are the underpinnings of language and cognitive development, emotional well-being, and social skills. The nurture and stimulation you provide at home to foster these connections should be extended and enhanced by what your child encounters every day in child care.

This Redleaf Guide covers critical issues that you will want to explore with your provider as you become partners in creating a stimulating and nurturing continuum of care and learning for your child. We at Redleaf Press wish you great success in building a collaborative relationship that is mutually enjoyable and productive for you, your provider, and most important, your child.

Eileen M. Nelson

Eileen Nelson
Director, Redleaf Press

Introduction

How to Be a Partner with Your Child Care Provider

Choosing a child care setting may be one of the most difficult things you'll ever do as a parent. It entails, after all, turning your child over, often for hours of every day, to another adult whom you don't really know. But you don't have to make your choice blindly. You can research the various child care settings available to you. You can visit centers and family child care settings and observe. You can interview the staff or the primary provider. You can talk to other families who use or have used a setting. You'll do all this because you want your child to have a good experience in child care, to have fun and learn, to form new skills and friendships. You want child care to be more than just something you have to do, to be more than a babysitter. You want child care to be both a pleasure and a growth experience for your child. (For more information, see Chapter 10 and the appendix, "Choosing Quality Child Care.")

Your effort doesn't stop with choosing a good setting, of course. The provider you choose becomes a very important person in your child's life, a partner, really, in raising your child in his or her early years. The very fact that the provider becomes so important may cause you some anxiety. No parent wants a child to become more attached to the provider than to his or her parents. You may feel a little sheepish if that thought has crossed your mind, but it's a pretty common anxiety. You really don't need to worry. Parents are, quite simply, the most important people in a child's life. (This is also true for guardians, such as grandparents, who become substitutes for the parents.) Although not an equal partner in parenting your child, the provider still plays a very important role. She can become a real partner in guiding and nurturing your child.

This book is about how to develop and cultivate a partnership with your provider. Developing a partnership with your child care provider requires skill, time, and commitment, but it is worth the effort. All of you—you, your child, and your provider—will have a better experience if that partnership is a strong one.

Why Is the Partnership Important?

Developing this partnership may feel like just one more job you shouldn't have to take on. Part of you may think, "I work hard enough. I'm paying good money to my provider to care for my child while I'm working, and everyone should just do their job." But, of course, putting your child in child care for the day isn't like dropping your car with the mechanic or sending your coat out for cleaning. You don't have to form a partnership with the mechanic in order for him to do a good job on your car. And you may not have to form a partnership with your provider in order for her to do a good job with your child either. But a partnership will enrich your child's experience and it will help your provider do the kind of job with your child that you want done.

Keep in mind that your provider probably has a lot to offer you. She may be trained in child development. She is probably accustomed to seeing and working with many different young children regularly. She can help you recognize the difference between issues that are related to general development and issues that are specific to your child. She can help you know what's appropriate to expect from a child the age of yours, and she can offer possible solutions to struggles you and your child may have.

Remember, too, that you have a lot to offer your provider. You know your child better than anyone else does. You know how to read your child's feelings better than anyone else does. You know her preferences and her abilities. You can give your provider important information and insights into your child's unique needs so your provider can do a better job.

Children get the most from their early education experience if a partnership exists between staff and family. When you and the provider collaborate, you both work in your child's best interests with the most information possible. Together, you can also offer your child more consistency, and both of you can reinforce what the other is trying to accomplish.

How Can You Build a Partnership?

One of the critical keys to working well with a provider is building a trusting relationship. Such a relationship is created through a lot of information sharing, respectful communication, and an understanding of each other's perspectives. Building a partnership also involves understanding the policies of the child care center or family child care setting, how the policies affect you and your child, what kind of flexibility you can expect from policies, and how you can work with them. It's also important to be aware of your values, to recognize when your values might be in conflict with the values reflected by your child care setting, and to be willing to find respectful ways to resolve any conflicts. You can build this partnership as you work together to support your child in her learning and behavioral development.

About This Book

This book was written to help bridge the difference in perspective between parents and early childhood teachers or child care providers. Other parents undoubtedly feel the same anxieties and face the same challenges that you do. So do providers, although perhaps from a different perspective. Understanding each other will help you feel more comfortable that your child is being cared for the way you want him to be.

The five sections of this book provide a framework for thinking through the factors that go into forming a partnership with your provider. These factors include the following:

- developing a trusting relationship with your provider
- understanding and working with program policies

- passing on your values to your child while respecting the values of other families in the program
- understanding child development issues
- ensuring that the child care setting is a good fit for your child

Each of these sections contains general information on the topic and a series of examples to make the information more concrete. The examples present hypothetical problems that allow you to see the issue both from the perspective of a parent and as a provider might look at it. Exploring the issues raised should help you gain confidence in solving problems.

Please note that, to reflect the reality that the child care profession is dominated by women, the provider is generally, though not always, referred to as "she" in this book. Fortunately, this is beginning to change. More men are entering the field of child care and early childhood education, giving children a broader experience of the many positive roles men can play in their lives.

Relationships

Chapter 1
Developing a Relationship with Your Provider

Many factors go into making a child care setting a good place for your child. You want it to be physically inviting, clean, and safe. You want the setting to have plenty of well-constructed and stimulating toys and healthy food. You want your child to have access to fun activities. Most important of all is the provider, or in the case of large centers, the staff who take care of your child. Your comfort and your child's comfort can depend on the quality of the relationship you build with your provider.

There will undoubtedly be moments when you question something your provider says or does. Even if your child care provider is an easy fit for you and you seem to look at the world in similar ways, there will sometimes be problems to solve and communication glitches to clear up.

Creating a positive relationship is more likely if you cultivate it. Here are some ideas to keep in mind as you work on building a trusting relationship with your provider:

- Share information.
- Be honest and direct.

- Understand the provider's perspective.
- Use the principles of active listening and respectful communication.
- Give providers the benefit of the doubt.
- Consult experienced parents to get other perspectives.
- Have reasonable expectations of your provider.
- Expect trustworthiness on both sides.
- Respect personal boundaries, yours and your provider's.
- Remember that the relationship you're building is in service to your child.

Tips for Building a Good Relationship

Joan thought she'd found the perfect child care provider. As she told a friend, "Terry is a wonderful provider. Tiffany loves her, but that's not the only reason I'm crazy about Terry. She's just a neat person! She really seems to care about me as well as Tiffany. She asks about my day, notices my mood, and shares funny stories about her own child. I feel so lucky to have Terry in our lives." Arriving at such a relationship didn't happen overnight. Joan had been taking her daughter to Terry's child care for two years, and there'd been some challenges along the way.

Think about your relationships with friends, with colleagues at work, with fellow committee or board members, with people in your community that do volunteer work with you. These relationships grow over time and their quality depends on their being nurtured. They require that you pay attention to what another person says and does, to who they are. Relationships require you to understand that others may see things differently than you do and that you be honest and tell people how you see things and what you need. You know that people have individual personalities, and you expect to interact with each person individually as the relationship requires.

Your child care provider, your child's preschool teacher, and any of the staff who work with your child at your child care center are all individuals with their own personalities, strengths, and weaknesses. Some providers are extroverts and are easy to interact with. Some are shy or contained. Some you feel an instant connection with and trust immediately; others take more time. Your provider doesn't have to be someone you feel personally drawn to or would like to have as a close friend. She only has to be someone who'll take good care of your child and support your child's physical, social, emotional, and cognitive development. The important thing is that you create a good working relationship. Here are some ways to lay the groundwork for such a relationship.

> Share Important Information

You can form a good partnership with your provider only if she has adequate information about your child, especially at the start of the relationship. Let your provider know about your child's temperament, whether she's shy or outgoing, whether transitions are difficult for her, whether or not she has tantrums frequently. Let your provider know if your child is very active, what his passions are, what his favorite toys are. Be up front with your provider if your child has any special needs. Knowing about them will help your provider prepare for working with your child. It will also help you know if the provider is equipped to meet the unique needs of your child.

Make information sharing a habit. If your child seems distressed about something that happened at child care, your provider needs to know. She cannot respond otherwise. Tell her about special events or changes at home that may affect your child. For instance, if friends are visiting from out of town for a week, your child may be unusually excited or tired. If you're under a lot of stress, your child could be feeling the impact of it, too, and you should let your provider know. You can choose how much detail to tell her, but at least let her know you're experiencing a challenge or crisis that may be affecting your child.

Your provider also needs to know when you have any special requests. If, for instance, you need to pick up your child half an hour later every Thursday, it's critical to find out whether this will work rather than assume the provider can meet this special need. You could end up with hurt feelings on both sides if you don't discuss this. Similarly, let your provider know as soon as you know that you'll be on vacation. It may influence her plans.

The provider should be giving you information as well. Most providers are conscientious about this, but they also can be busy or preoccupied and forget to tell you something. Don't be afraid to ask. It's also possible that your provider may feel nervous about telling you something that happened, such as that the children were inadvertently exposed to the flu. She may be afraid you'll think she or her center has been neglectful.

One evening, after Tiffany had been in Terry's child care just a few weeks, she became very upset as she talked to her mother about that afternoon's naptime. Joan couldn't understand what her daughter was upset about, so she called Terry. Joan learned that Terry had let Tiffany take her favorite teddy bear to the library and somehow the bear got left behind. Terry acknowledged that she should have told Joan about it, but she'd been afraid Joan might think she was careless, and she'd hoped to retrieve the bear before it became a problem. This open conversation helped Joan and Terry take a step toward a better relationship early on.

You have a right to know what's happening to and around your child while he's in child care. You need to judge for yourself whether something that's occurred is a threat to your child or otherwise is of concern to you. In addition, you may need to help your child understand something he's experienced at child care. If you feel your provider isn't being forthcoming with you, or if she'd failed to tell you about a significant event, you should discuss it with her. Be forthright, and approach the conversation with an open attitude. Bear in mind, however, that a provider is not free to give you confidential information about another child. Say, for example, that a child has an allergic reaction to a bee bite in front of your child and your child finds it frightening. You can tell your provider that you'd appreciate knowing about such things, but you cannot expect her to tell you anything specific about the nature of the child's allergies. Only that child's parents can decide when and to whom such information can be given.

If your provider tells you about your child's misbehavior, don't be afraid to ask for clarification. You may wonder whether she's asking you to discipline your child at home for something he did during the day. You need to be clear on this point. You can support your provider's rules by talking with your child, by reading relevant books to him, or through dramatic play, but disciplining him at the end of the day for something he did earlier in child care probably wouldn't make sense to him and so would not be effective.

>Be Honest and Direct

If questions or issues arise that are disturbing to you, don't remain silent about them. Arrange a mutually convenient time to talk with your provider and have an open, honest, respectful conversation. If you have what you feel may be a difficult conversation ahead of you, try to keep the points that follow in mind.

- Maintain a calm demeanor even if you're nervous.
- Don't bring up the issue when your child is nearby. You don't want to risk having your child overhear. In addition, if your child reacts to the tension between you and your provider, the whole situation may escalate.
- Make arrangements for follow-up conversation if necessary. Perhaps your provider will need time to digest what you've brought up. Suggest that you set up a time to talk again.

> Understand That the Provider Has a Different Perspective

Perhaps your provider has said no to requests that seem perfectly reasonable to you, a situation that can be enormously frustrating. In another instance that occurred early in her relationship with her child care provider, Joan and her husband and three children were leaving on a Tuesday evening to visit her parents. It was a four-hour flight, and Tiffany was a restless child. She hated being in confined spaces for any length of time. Joan wanted Tiffany to sleep on the airplane, so she asked Terry to let Tiffany skip her nap Tuesday afternoon.

Terry balked. Since she made all her phone calls while the children were sleeping, it would be difficult having Tiffany stay up. She also said Tiffany was generally really tired by naptime, and she wasn't sure she could keep her awake. And besides, other children would probably want to skip naptime if Tiffany did.

Joan was irritated. She wondered what the big deal was. Couldn't Terry just put Tiffany in front of a video this one time while she made her phone calls? Couldn't she just tell the other children they had to take their nap no matter what Tiffany did? After all, Terry wasn't the one who was going to have to sit by a cranky kid during that plane ride.

Joan was missing the fact that her provider had a different perspective than she did. It was Joan's job to think about the needs of her family. It was Terry's job to balance the needs of all the children and the program as a whole. She knew from experience that allowing one child to skip naptime could be very disruptive, something Joan didn't understand. Also, Terry had a number of administrative tasks to do, and if she didn't do them during naptime she had to use her personal time in the evening on them. This was another point Joan didn't appreciate until after she and Terry had a phone conversation later that day. They were able to work out a solution. Joan hired a high-school student whom Tiffany knew to come over during naptime and take Tiffany to the park.

You'll be well on your way to building a trusting relationship if you give your provider all the information she needs to do a good job, and if you try to understand her perspective when it differs from yours. Try to keep an open mind and think about how your request might affect the whole group of children, the program, and the provider.

> Use Active Listening and Respectful Communication

Respectful communication is probably the single most important element in building a good relationship with your provider. Joan's relationship with her provider could have suffered a significant setback when Terry balked at keeping Tiffany up during her naptime that particular Tuesday. It had felt so unreasonable to Joan. She decided to call a friend whose children were older, and her friend urged her to talk it over with Terry, to keep an open mind and see if they couldn't find a solution. Joan and her husband had gone through some marriage counseling that had taught them both a lot about improving their own relationship through open and respectful communication. She decided to apply what she'd learned to her relationship with Terry.

Good communication contributes to problem solving, increases trust, and dissolves tension. Children notice the relationships between the important people in their lives—especially those between authority figures such as their parents and teachers or child care providers—and being aware of tension or conflict can upset them. Along with building a trusting relationship, good communication provides a powerful model for your child. Imagine your delight should your child use the respectful communication techniques she's learned watching you to interact with you or her siblings or her friends.

It would seem that good communication skills should be second nature. After all, you've been talking for how many years now? And getting along fine in this world? Still, it can be helpful to articulate and be purposeful about our communication. Here are some elements of respectful communication that you need to employ.

- Listen attentively. Don't interrupt. Let your provider finish her thought before you start in on your own again. Hear the feelings that drive the words. For instance, sometimes fear sounds like anger, and if you're listening attentively, you can notice this.

- Demonstrate that you understand. This is called reflective listening, responding to the other person in a way that shows you heard and understood what they had to say. If phrases such as "I hear you saying . . ." or "It sounds like . . ." feel stilted to you, find a way of expressing these ideas that fits you. You might say, "I wonder if . . ." or "Do you feel . . ." as other ways to reflect what your provider tells you.

- Show others that you understand their perspective. When you show your provider that you understand her perspective, she may be more open to working with you to find a solution. And you'll have the opportunity to correct your assumptions if you've read a situation wrong. You might, for example, think your provider is angry about something when she's actually worried. If you don't know, you have to ask.

- Avoid blaming the other person. Most people get defensive and have difficulty hearing what another person has to say when they feel attacked. It may seem perfectly obvious to you that your provider should understand your concern and react professionally. Yet, like you, she has personal feelings wrapped up in her job and may not always be able to separate them from the issue at hand.

- Keep the conversation on track. If your provider gets defensive and accuses you of something else, don't go there. You can say, "We can talk about that as well, but right now we need to find a solution for this issue that will work for both of us."

- Don't generalize. Avoid saying "you always" or "you never." Generalizing behavior makes people feel judged and defensive. For instance, instead of saying, "You never warn Carlos that I'll be here to pick him up soon," you might say, "Last week I arrived three times to find that Carlos hadn't started getting ready to go home yet, and it's happened two times this week. Then it takes me twice as long to get him moving. I really need him to have some warning." Avoid negative, shaming, and emotionally charged words such as rude, disrespectful, selfish, neglectful, incompetent, or other words you wouldn't like used to describe you.

When you've found a solution, say it out loud again to make sure you both heard the same thing. Restating is a way of clarifying and making sure that you've understood each other. Joan said, "So I'll ask the babysitter to be here at two thirty in the afternoon, and she'll take Tiffany to the park for an hour and a half." Terry said, "Great. That should work out perfectly. And actually, the sitter could return her after an hour. Some of the children are starting to get up by that time."

> Give the Provider the Benefit of the Doubt

Most of the time it's safe to assume that your provider has the best interests of your child at heart and wants you to be satisfied with the care she gives your child. In other words, you can assume her intentions are good. A case in point: Mai's mother, Phua, was surprised and upset when Mai showed up with the child care center's hamster for the weekend. It was a difficult weekend to have the pet, for a group of out-of-town relatives was staying with them. Her first response was to be annoyed at her provider. "What does she think she's doing, sending home the hamster without my permission?" Then she decided she'd better check into what had happened. It turned out the provider had told Phua about the children having an opportunity to bring the hamster home on weekends and had asked if she'd like Mai to do that. Phua, who didn't understand English very well, had accidentally agreed to this particular weekend. Fortunately, Phua didn't assume the provider had ignored her wishes. After they had their conversation, both realized they needed to be more careful to check out what each of them had understood.

Lilian Katz, noted expert on both early childhood and teacher education, believes all of us have a tendency at times to attribute our own mistakes to circumstances (traffic was bad, clocks were wrong) and other people's mistakes to character flaws (she's flaky, she comes late because she likes to make an entrance) (NAEYC Annual Conference, 1995, Washington, D.C., "The Use of NAEYC's Code of Ethical Conduct within Child Care Facilities"). Assuming people have positive intentions changes this tendency to attribute mistakes to character flaws and concentrates our attention on the circumstances at hand. Positive expectations and a strong sense of forgiveness count for much when it comes to communicating.

>Consult Experienced Parents

If you feel you need to talk with your provider about a difficult subject you haven't been faced with before, you might want to talk it through with another parent. It needn't be a parent with a child in the same program, but it's helpful if it's a parent who has some experience with child care and has faced a similar situation.

Talk about how you'll open the conversation, how you'll want to approach the subject. You'll need to be tactful, of course, and you'll want to begin the dialogue in a way that isn't blaming or critical. If you feel your provider isn't hearing what you have to say, you need to think about what you can say and how you can say it. At the same time, you'll need to remain aware of listening to what your provider has to say. And finally, you'll need to decide whether you want your child's other parent to be with you during the discussion.

Experienced parents also can give you some perspective on what you might reasonably expect in a child care setting. If you're feeling anxious about the way a provider has responded to a concern, or about the way she's handling a particular situation, other parents can give you feedback that can let you put the incident into perspective. Maybe what you're concerned about isn't as big a deal as you think it is. Or maybe it is, and you really need to do something.

>Have Reasonable Expectations of the Provider

Remember that your provider is working under time constraints and has to be alert to the needs of all the children in her care, so she can't take a lot of time to chat whenever you happen to be there. Find a way to communicate that works for both of you, perhaps quick conversations at the beginning of the day, or phone calls in the evening, or e-mail. If you're sensitive to the demands on her time, she'll be more open to talking with you.

Initially, when Joan picked up her daughter, she felt frustrated over not getting as much detail as she wanted about Tiffany's day. But once Joan understood how distracting it was for Terry to try to focus on her while all the children were still there, and once Terry understood how important it was to Joan to get more specific information, they were able to work out a compromise that served them better and better as time went on. They had a phone conversation once a week while the children napped, and soon Joan had such a good sense of what

Tiffany's days were like that her need for detailed information lessened.

Don't expect perfection. Sometimes parents see their provider as an expert who can tell them how to solve difficulties with their child, and they expect to hear advice that's going to work. Try to remember that, although your provider may well have a lot of child development information and insight into your child, she can't solve your problems; she can only give you information and partner with you in finding solutions.

>Expect Trustworthiness on Both Sides

You and your provider need to be able to trust each other to follow through on what you say you'll do. For instance, if your provider says she'll give your child a five-minute warning before you come, you should be able to count on that. By the same token, if your provider has a firm pickup time, you should not be chronically late. If you promise to supply extra clothing, do so. If you disclose information about your child to the provider, you should be able to count on her keeping it confidential. It can be helpful if you tell your provider when a piece of information feels especially sensitive to you.

>Respect Personal Boundaries

Entrusting your child to another adult can feel pretty intimate. For example, you may talk with your provider about difficulties you're facing with your child, which is perfectly appropriate. This is what your partnership is about. But such conversation can also slip over into talking about things you feel vulnerable about, maybe problems in your home or your marriage or with other family members that are having an impact on your child. Sometimes parents find themselves wanting their provider to take care of them emotionally or to become their friend. The fact that relationships with family child care providers are informal makes them especially susceptible to this kind of intimacy.

You may form a connection with a provider that goes beyond the professional boundaries of your relationship, and this may be fine. It's also possible that a provider won't be open to this, even though you thought she would be. When you share personal information and work together on issues concerning your child that are emotionally charged, your relationship with your provider can be confusing. You might feel that a provider is offering a more intimate relationship than she is, or you may be asking for a more intimate relationship than she's comfortable with. She may like you a great deal but prefer not to form friendships with parents. Or she may simply have too much going on in her life at a particular time. It could also go the other way; a provider could begin to disclose more personal information to you than you want to hear. Be aware of your personal boundaries and thoughtful about what personal information you choose to disclose.

>Remember That the Relationship Is in Service to Your Child

As your child spends months and even years with a provider, you may become closer to the provider. But remember that the primary focus must be your child's needs. A child can easily get pushed out of the way when adults are enjoying each other. And sometimes you may need to challenge your provider about your child's care, and your personal relationship with the provider should not get in the way. Whether your relationship with the provider is easy or challenging, remember that the point of the relationship is to provide the best possible guidance and care for your child. Make your child the priority in cultivating a partnership with your provider.

• • •

Points to Remember and Discuss

- Of all the factors in a child care setting that contribute to the welfare of your child, the provider is probably the most important.
- Cultivating an open, collaborative relationship with a provider allows both the parents and the provider to give a child the best possible care.
- It helps to build a good relationship if you are direct and honest in sharing your concerns while remaining respectful of differences and holding reasonable expectations.
- Practicing good basic listening skills and respecting your provider's perspective will help in reaching compromises and resolving differences.
- Showing appreciation to your provider regularly goes a long way toward building goodwill.
- It is essential that you both respect personal boundaries and are clear and consistent in your communication.

Chapter 2
Challenges to Relationship

You can have all the empathy in the world, bend over backward to understand your provider's perspective, and work hard at direct respectful communication; still, you more than likely will experience some challenging situations. This chapter presents examples of potentially disruptive situations in which parents and providers were able to increase the trust in their relationship by collaborating to find solutions.

When Your Sense of Trust Is Disturbed

When Maria arrived at the child care center, Rosa already had her snowsuit and boots on. That was a welcome relief for Maria, who, tired at the end of a long workday, wasn't looking forward to wrestling Rosa into her outdoor clothes. But she found an unwelcome surprise when they got home and she helped Rosa out of her snowsuit.

Rosa had arrived at the center that morning in a pair of blue jeans and a pink sweater. Now she was wearing brown corduroy pants and a long-sleeved white shirt.

"Whose clothes are those?" Maria asked. Rosa just looked at her mother with a puzzled expression. Maria tried again. "Why don't you have your own clothes on?"

"I don't know," Rosa said, as she took off after her cat.

Maria was upset and puzzled. She'd left an additional outfit at child care for Rosa. Why didn't the provider use that? Were Rosa's clothes ruined and the provider didn't tell her? She didn't have the kind of money to be replacing whole outfits at the drop of a hat. Did the provider disapprove of the way she dressed Rosa? Now she'd have to make sure she got those clothes washed and back to the provider. What a nuisance. And what if something got ruined in the washer? Would she be responsible for buying new clothes?

When Maria's sister dropped by after dinner, Maria told her that Rosa had come home wearing some stranger's clothing, even someone else's underwear. Her sister frowned. "That's weird," she said. "Why was someone messing with her underwear? Do you think something bad could have happened to her? What do you know about this provider, anyway?" Maria hadn't even considered inappropriate touching, but now she wondered about that too.

Maria muttered to herself while she fixed lunches for the next day. Her sister was always thinking the worst thing imaginable. She wasn't going to go there. But what if . . . She couldn't stop wondering. Did the provider disapprove of the way she dressed Rosa? Could it possibly have been something worse? After the children were in bed, Maria talked it over with her husband. He suggested she just come right out and ask the provider what happened. "You've got a right to know," he said.

When Maria told her provider the next day that she wanted to talk with her, the provider asked if she could give her a call at home. Maria started the conversation that evening with a direct question. "Why did Rosa come home in someone else's clothes yesterday? I asked her, but she told me she didn't know."

"I'm sorry," the provider said. "I should have told you. Things were so hectic when you picked up Rosa that I forgot to mention it." Rosa had wet herself, the provider explained. She was embarrassed by her accident and refused to put on the extra clothing Maria had sent. She'd been able to persuade Rosa to cooperate in getting dressed again only after Rosa spied the Cinderella underwear and some extra clothing the provider kept in a dresser drawer. The provider decided to just let her use that instead.

Maria breathed a sigh of relief. A perfectly logical explanation. She knew Rosa didn't like the set of extra clothes she'd sent. In fact, one of the reasons she'd sent them was that they wouldn't be missed at home. "Thank you," she said. "But you know, I gotta tell you, I'm really more comfortable with Rosa wearing her own clothes. Maybe I need to send an extra set that Rosa actually likes."

"That's a great idea," the provider said.

Developing trust is often the first challenge to a relationship between a parent and a provider. It's scary to trust your young child to someone else's care, especially if your child can't speak for herself yet. You have every right to check out any questions that arise. In fact, you need to. Trust will come over time as the provider proves trustworthy and your questions are answered. Eventually you should be able to trust that the provider cares about and for your child, likes your child, and understands her well enough to meet her needs.

It's easy to imagine the worst, but jumping to conclusions doesn't help you develop a workable relationship with a provider. Even more important, it doesn't help your child. In this case, Maria resisted her sister's impulse to jump to a catastrophic conclusion. Still, so it wouldn't keep nagging at her, she asked the question she needed to ask. Direct and immediate communication prevented a straightforward incident from becoming an issue that destroyed trust between the provider and the parent.

Maria was also careful not to accuse. She could have said, "What's the matter? Rosa's clothes aren't good enough for you?" Or, "I need to know what's going on over there. Why are you putting my daughter in someone else's underwear?" Such blaming overtones probably would have made the provider defensive. A straightforward, direct question is much more apt to elicit a straightforward, honest answer. Just as important, direct and respectful questions lay the foundation for building a good working relationship.

Maria, like many parents, worried about sexual abuse when her sister raised the specter. Although sexual abuse is an especially daunting worry for parents, it rarely occurs in child care settings. A child is actually much more apt to be touched inappropriately or otherwise abused by an adult he knows, a relative, a neighbor, or a friend. Still, such abuse is an important possibility to be aware of, and there might come a time when you would want to look at it closely. We'll discuss this topic in more depth in Chapter 4.

If you feel you don't consistently get information about the things that as a parent you want to know— what food your child is eating, perhaps, or what naptime arrangements are like, or how your child reacts to out- ings—ask for more information. Let your provider know that communication with her is important to you. You may need to plan with your provider for the best ways and times to get information. As mentioned in Chapter 1, pick-up time can be very busy, and the provider is responsible for all the children in her care. A phone call or e-mail or a monthly conversation are good alterna- tives. Be open to ideas.

Sometimes fathers find it more difficult to develop a relationship because they feel so outnumbered by moth- ers or they feel left out of the loop. This is less a problem as time goes on and more fathers become more involved in their young children's lives. If you are a father and find that a provider or preschool teacher gravitates to the mothers or is quicker to give them information, don't be afraid to ask that you be included. If you find yourself thinking something like "She doesn't think I'm as impor- tant as the mothers," try to pull yourself out of this defensive posture. If the provider is gravitating toward the mothers, it may well be a habit learned over years of having the mothers be the ones who form relationships. Just remind her that you want to be an active partner too. You can say, "It helps me feel more secure when I get information about what happens while my daughter's here. I love hearing about her day. So I'm happy for any information you can give me."

Parents who are separated or divorced, especially non-custodial parents, can find themselves anxious about developing a relationship with a provider. But it's important for both the custodial and the noncustodial parent to form a partnership with the provider. It can be tempting to let conflict between you and your child's other parent intrude on the child care setting, perhaps because one parent wants to be recognized as the more responsible or important parent, or worries about equality and aggressively demands it. When this happens, children will feel the tension that results, and the child care setting will feel a little less secure or safe for them. The provider may feel confused about what she should be saying to whom. Both parents have a right to information about the child care setting and what happens there, and both need to ask their questions in a way that doesn't spill the conflict with the other parent onto the provider. Both need to remain respectful and interested.

When You Don't Feel Welcome

Helen had been taking her son, Derrick, to the Southside Family Center for two months. She often tried to strike up a conversation with Shandra, the provider, when she picked up Derrick. "How was your day?" she'd ask. Or, "I can't wait until this weekend. What a hard week it's been at work. What are you doing for the weekend?"

Shandra was polite but reticent. She might answer, "I don't have much planned," and then turn away to a task that needed doing. This was uncomfortable for Helen. And she didn't feel particularly welcome.

Helen worked full time, but when she had a day off coming up, she thought it would be fun to spend the morning at the center. She wanted to know people a bit better and to see what it was like for Derrick. She was sure Shandra would welcome the help. But when she mentioned the possibility, Shandra said, "Thanks, but we're fine here. I don't really need any help."

Helen's feelings were hurt. She felt unwanted, and she wondered why. She thought Shandra would be happy to have help. "You sure?" she asked. "It wouldn't be any trouble."

"No, really. It's okay."

When she got home, Helen called her friend Marian to talk over what had happened. Marian had a six-year-old and an eight-year-old who'd both been in child care when they were younger. Surely, Helen thought, her friend could help her figure out what to do, or at least help her to not feel so bad.

Her friend laughed. "Oh, girlfriend, do I know that one." Marian told Helen about an experience she'd had when her eight-year-old first started child care. She'd actually had a big fight with her provider after being told she didn't need to hang around so much. Fortunately, they were able to work things out and her daughter remained in that center. "You know what it turned out to be?" Marian asked.

"Enlighten me."

"I was amazed. It turned out the provider thought I was trying to spy on her! She was new, and she was worried she wasn't doing a good enough job." Marian described to Helen how the two of them had sat down with the center director and talked until they both had a better understanding of each other.

Sometimes parents don't feel welcome in the child care setting. But, with few exceptions—on days when there's special programming, perhaps, or when space restrictions apply—you should be allowed access at any time. You have every right to know what's happening in your child's environment at any time. But it's also important that you try to understand why a provider is reacting to you in a certain way. If you're trying to make conversation at pick-up time and the provider is short with you, if you're searching for a way to make a connection and not finding it, you may feel confused. You may wonder why a provider would act like that. You may even think she doesn't like you.

Providers feel an enormous responsibility for the children in their care. They often feel a need to be constantly vigilant. Because they want to keep track of every child, they may be constantly roving the room with their eyes while you're talking to them. It's quite unlike going to a friend's house and watching a few children while the two of you talk. If you're feeling like it's impossible to find a time to connect, ask your provider when would be a good time for a conversation.

It may also surprise you to know that providers feel anxious about being judged by parents. If you, like Maria, are concerned about what your provider thinks of you and your parenting, she probably feels a similar concern about your opinion. When a parent walks into the room, a provider often begins to look at the children she's watching through the parent's eyes. Her behavior may become more stilted as she worries about how it looks to the parent when Carrie shoves Judy away from the sandbox or Jimmy won't respond when asked to pick up a toy. If you appreciate the job your provider is doing, let her know that. It will be easier for the two of you to form a good working relationship if one of you isn't feeling judged by the other.

When you do help in the classroom, ask the teacher or provider what she needs from you. Be willing to do some of the drudgery. Fetch things. Cut out materials for an art project. Pick up the paper scraps from the floor. Most providers will welcome the help, especially if they can relax, knowing you're there because you want to partner with them, not judge them.

When an Assessment Is Recommended for Your Child

Tim had been attending Twin Pines Early Childhood Learning Center for a couple of months before his parents had their first parent-teacher conference. John and

Linda liked the center a lot. They thought the staff was terrific, and the staff seemed to enjoy Tim. John dropped Tim at the center each morning and was generally the one who picked him up at the end of the day. On a few occasions, his teacher had mentioned to John that Tim wasn't catching on to some of the center's routines as quickly as they'd expected. While John and Linda were glad the staff was being so attentive, they also found hearing this unsettling. They hoped the staff wasn't taking too critical a view of Tim.

When John and Linda arrived for their parent-teacher conference, they found both the teacher and the center director waiting for them. The director explained that there was a possibility Tim wasn't quite on track developmentally. They wanted to have him screened. John and Linda asked a lot of questions, said how glad they were that the teacher was keeping such a close eye on Tim, and signed the papers giving permission for the screening.

Even though Tim's teacher had mentioned her concerns to John a few times, the request for screening took both parents by surprise. As they drove home, they discussed how they were feeling. "What do you think this means?" John asked.

"I can't believe there's anything seriously wrong with Tim," Linda answered. "We would have noticed something at home."

They decided to call John's sister, who was a psychologist. "Don't worry about Tim," she reassured them. "People push kids too hard these days, expect too much of them too soon. Tim doesn't need any labels. Let him develop at his own pace."

The more they thought and talked about it as the evening wore on, the more concerned John and Linda became. "I don't know," Linda said. "Maybe that center's not the right place for Tim. Let's call your mom and see if she can watch Tim for a few days while we look for another place."

Since one of the greatest parental fears is that something's wrong with their child, a request for an assessment raises frightening questions. Parents dream about their children's future. They picture them growing up, imagine what kind of career they might choose, whom they might marry, what their passions will be. If their child develops problems along the way, this dream is disturbed and may even be lost. Parents also feel guilty. Did they miss something important for their child? Did they do something wrong? Was it the wine I drank occasionally at dinner when I was pregnant? Was it because I went back to work too soon?

A request for an assessment doesn't necessarily mean that your child has a problem. Teachers and child care providers generally want to err on the side of caution, but many of them are schooled in recognizing developmental problems and feel pressure to identify problems so they can be addressed as early as possible. Teachers and providers feel their own sense of responsibility and guilt if they miss something important. They typically want to make sure nothing has been missed on their watch.

John's sister had raised another issue that parents often have strong feelings about. Both parents and professionals worry about children being given a label that will follow them through school and cause others to pigeonhole them. The concern, of course, is that the label may color people's perception of a child.

The bottom line is that you as the parent are the ultimate decision maker. You're the one who'll decide whether your child has an assessment, and you'll decide what you want to do with any information you get from an assessment. At the same time, you'll gain the great benefit of knowing early on if your child has some kind of problem.

Tim's teacher called John and Linda when Tim didn't show up at the center the next day. She asked what had happened. Linda took a deep breath and decided to just put it out there. "John's sister is a psychologist. She doesn't think there's anything wrong with Tim, and she thinks the center may be jumping to conclusions. We don't want Tim labeled."

The teacher reassured Linda that the ultimate decision-making power would rest with her and her husband, and that she shared their concern about labels. "We don't know that there's anything wrong with Tim. We just want to be careful. You certainly don't have to do anything you don't want to do. How about if we just talk this over a bit more?"

John and Linda decided to meet again with the teacher and the center director. They felt reassured that the school would be respectful of their input and decisions. "I'm glad you were up front with them about how we felt," John told his wife. "You opened a good dialogue."

Tim was screened, taken to a child psychologist for a more complete assessment, and a learning disorder was identified. The psychologist outlined for John and Linda ways that Tim could be supported at home and at school so his learning disorder wouldn't slow him down. His parents were able to partner with the center staff in supporting Tim.

If you're faced with a request for a screening or assessment, enlist your provider as a partner in taking a closer look at your child and in providing any special support that might be necessary. Although it may feel frightening, remember that a request for a screening is not a conclusion that your child has a problem. And remember that, with early identification and support, many problems can be overcome. Above all, remember that as the parent you will remain in charge.

• • •

Points to Remember and Discuss

- It's common for parents to have anxieties at some point about something going on in their child care setting they disagree with or don't understand.
- When problems and misunderstandings arise it's doubly important to remain open and work for solutions in the context of sustaining a trusting relationship with your provider.
- You need to be direct and honest about concerns such as

not feeling welcome at child care. At the same time, remain willing to listen to what your provider has to say and to try to understand her perspective.

- A request for a professional assessment doesn't imply criticism of you or your child. Obtaining an assessment can be a positive time during which you collaborate with your provider in the best interest of your child.

Policies

Chapter 3
Policies That Work for Families

"I'm so annoyed at Billy's teacher. Billy loves that new truck his grandpa gave him for his birthday, and she won't let him bring it with him. 'It's policy,' she says. Why would they have such a stupid policy anyway?"

You may have had feelings about your child's preschool or child care setting that are similar to this mother's. A child care center's policies should serve families and their children well, but this isn't always the case. And even the best policies can be frustrating at times.

The Point of Policies

Policies for child care programs are established for various reasons. They exist to protect the health and welfare of the children. They exist to protect staff as well. Policies may be in place to help the provider manage groups of children, or they may have been created in response to a specific problem that occurred in the past. Policies are usually established in the hope of making things work better for the children, the parents, and the program.

When you're selecting a child care setting, it's wise to ask about their policies. If there are written policies, ask for a copy. It's better to know before enrollment if there are policies that won't work for you or your child. If a particular policy poses a problem for you, ask the provider whether an exception might be allowed in your case or if there's leeway to negotiate a compromise.

Policies generally are more flexible in a family child care setting. A family child care provider need not be concerned about consistency among multiple classrooms or about whether employees receive similar treatment. She is self-employed and has the latitude to make her own decisions. In contrast, a provider in a child care center answers to an administrator or director, who may, in turn, need to consult a board of directors or a parent company on issues such as exceptions to a policy. Another issue for centers is the more difficult logistics of making changes. For instance, a family child care provider may find it relatively easy to substitute another food if a parent tells her his child cannot eat wheat. A center that has its food catered, however, would have to work with its caterer to figure out a solution.

Some aspects of policies are dictated by external regulations. In most states, child care providers, centers, and preschools are licensed, and policies about health and safety are affected by licensing standards. The National Association for the Education of Young Children (NAEYC) has a voluntary accreditation system. Setting policies that are in conflict with NAEYC criteria limits the ability to become an accredited program. Most programs are responsible for adhering to the Americans with Disabilities Act (ADA). Creating policies that exclude children and staff with special needs is likely to be in conflict with this law.

If you think that a policy at your child's center is unreasonable or is detrimental to the children, you can talk with your provider or an administrator. Policies generally are put in place for good reasons, but sometimes a policy has outlived its usefulness. Ask about the reasons for the policy; get a better understanding of it. You may decide it's important after all and you can live with it. Or maybe you won't see it that way. Perhaps you can get involved in the process that is set up for creating or modifying policies.

Some Typical Policies

Considered below are a few areas in which providers generally have similar policies.

> Sick Child Policies

Sick child policies are in place to protect your child from catching illnesses from other children. They aren't fool-proof, of course. Despite the best efforts of parents, providers, and administrators, children still catch colds and get the flu at child care. Although policies may be frustrating when it's your child who can't attend, they still do benefit your child in the long run.

Children generally are not allowed to attend child care when they have a temperature of 100 degrees Fahrenheit or higher or when they have active colored mucus, wet coughs, or pus in their eyes. State legal requirements play a role in this area of policy development. Many states require that children be immunized before they can attend certain programs. Sometimes processes are developed for allowing exceptions. If immunization is a concern for you, ask your provider about it.

It is reasonable to expect notification if your child has been exposed to a contagious disease at child care. Most programs will do this, either through letters or in notes sent home in children's backpacks, or simply through a conversation.

If your child has special medical needs, you'll want to be especially attentive to health and medical policies. Program policy regarding giving medications can vary considerably. For instance, many programs will not give medications such as aspirin, cough medicine, etc., because by giving medicine without a doctor's prescription, they may be assuming liability. Some states will allow EpiPens, a lifesaving injection for people allergic to substances such as bee stings, to be administered only by programs with a nurse on staff. If your child needs this medication, you'll have to find a program that will administer it or a program close enough to your job that you could quickly get there and administer it yourself. It is your job as a parent to find a program that is safe for your child.

The two main frustrations parents tend to experience with sick child policies are really opposite sides of the same coin. Either the policy is too lax and their children are getting exposed to diseases, or the policy is too strict and excludes their children when they're just a little under the weather and shouldn't have to stay home.

Sometimes a provider will err on the side of caution and exclude your child for having a cold when you know his runny nose and red eyes are due to an allergy. And sometimes a provider will be reluctant to take your child even though she's been on antibiotics for twenty-four hours. The American Academy of Pediatrics (AAP) issues recommendations for child care centers. If you're concerned about whether a provider's policy or a particular response is reasonable, check the academy's guidelines. You can find them in *Caring for Our Children: National Health and Safety Performance Standards: Guidelines for Out-of-Home Child Care Programs*, 2nd Edition (American Academy of Pediatrics, American Public Health Association, and National Resource Center for Health and Safety in Child Care, 2002) at your library or for purchase online through the AAP bookstore at www.aap.org/.

Many programs and providers require a letter from a doctor in order to make exceptions to their sick child policies. Remember that this has nothing to do with whether they trust you; they need to cover themselves legally.

> Schedule Policies

When it comes to schedules, centers and family child care providers often have similar policies. They tend to have strict guidelines for drop-off and pick-up time, although some programs offer extended care for an additional fee. It may feel unreasonable to you that you can't make a quick run into the grocery store before picking up your child, but if it means you'll be a few minutes late, it's a problem.

Parents may wonder what the big deal is if they're five or ten minutes late. They wonder why they have to watch the clock so closely. But people's concept of time varies by individual and by culture. Strict adherence to the clock is a Western concept, and cultural differences often come into play here.

Programs may have no choice but to have strict pick-up times. The staff may be members of unions that require a limit on the number of hours worked. Accrediting bodies that certify the quality of programs also may require that teachers work with children only a certain number of hours.

Just as important are the personal reasons. Providers often have children of their own. If you're late picking up your child, the provider will be late picking up her child. This can lead to resentment by even the most generous and flexible provider. One of the most effective things you can do to maintain a positive relationship with your provider is to arrive on time. And if you can't avoid being late, let her know ahead of time, apologize, and offer to compensate her. Late fees generally run about $1 per minute. Since everybody's watch is set to a slightly different time, go by the clock at your child care setting.

Last but certainly not least is the impact being late has on your child. Children tend to get anxious if all the other children have been picked up and they're still waiting, wondering where Mom, Dad, or Grandma is. Your provider can offer your child reassurance, but it will be easier for her to do that if you've notified her ahead of time. She won't then be passing on to your child any anxiety she may feel as she wonders where you are, when you're coming, and what may have happened.

> Clothing Policies

Some programs set limits on types of clothing allowed. For instance, Waldorf schools usually don't allow children to wear anything that is visibly commercial. Your son probably can't wear a T-shirt with Pokémon on the front to a Waldorf school. Some programs require that specific clothing be worn, for example, closed-toe shoes to protect children's feet, shorts under dresses to protect girls' modesty, or underwear to protect children's hygiene. Some programs do not want children to wear party shoes. The reason a program may object is that party shoes can keep a child from being as active as she might otherwise be, and they also may not be safe for outdoor play. If it's easier to get your child out the door wearing her party shoes, go ahead and let her. But bring other shoes along. It can be valuable to keep a change of clothing at child care, even if your child is toilet trained, for those times when she gets soaked during water play or muddy playing outdoors.

Clothing policies may vary, but most child care settings will not be responsible for seeing that children's clothing remains clean and unstained. Providers want children to be free to explore and learn, and that often involves taking spills and getting dirty. Programs may have smocks available for children to wear, but a provider may not insist a smock be worn if it means the child will refuse to do an activity. You might find that frustrating, especially if your child comes home with a stain on a new shirt, so it's best not to send your child in clothing that's precious to you.

Children with Special Needs

Many programs include children who have special needs. Although a program may value the opportunity to include such a child, it generally is not a choice. The Americans with Disabilities Act makes it illegal for programs to exclude children with special needs.

There are some exceptions. If meeting a special need would inhibit the purpose of the program, it would be excepted. For instance, if the center is a preschool on a farm, a parent could not enroll a child allergic to animals and expect the program to remove all the animals. But, unless it can be demonstrated that hiring additional teachers would put the program in jeopardy, a program cannot claim it doesn't have enough teachers to meet a child's need for extra support. For more information, you can read *Commonly Asked Questions about Child Care Centers and the Americans with Disabilities Act*. You can find it on the U.S. Department of Justice's Internet site. The specific address for this publication is www.ada.gov/childq&a.htm.

Parents who worry about having children with special needs in their own child's program may be pleasantly surprised to discover that their child benefits from being with children who have disabilities. They might, for instance, find that their child learns empathy by spending time with a child who has special needs. One family had their youngest child, a little boy who'd often experienced the world as revolving around him, in a center when a child with Down syndrome began attending. The boy's parents were concerned that providers would be forced to spend so much time with Paul that their son would be neglected. Arriving to pick up his son one afternoon, the father observed some of the children patting Paul on the top of his head. He then heard his own son say to the other children, "Don't touch him like that. He's not a dog." The father realized that learning such empathy was a gift to his three-year-old. Don't assume that the presence of children with special needs will take anything away from your child.

Programs are restricted from divulging information regarding children with special needs. You can't expect them, for instance, to tell you a child's diagnosis. Data privacy laws prohibit this.

• • •

Points to Remember and Discuss

- Policies exist to protect both the programs and the families that participate in them.
- There is a wide variation in policies among settings, and some settings may be more flexible than others.
- It may be possible to get a written copy of your child care's policies. Talk through them with your provider. If you're enrolling your child in a new setting, check out the

policies before you commit. You need to be sure policies are compatible with your expectations and needs.

- You need to talk with your provider and be especially clear about illness, schedules and late fees, clothing, and special needs policies.

- It's important to try to understand the perspective of the center or home if you find a policy difficult. Try to work with the provider to make changes if you feel a policy is unnecessary or even detrimental to your child.

Chapter 4
Policy Discomforts

Even though policies generally are put in place for good reasons, they may not always make sense for your child. And sometimes, if you take a deeper look at them, you may find that they do make good sense. Here are some examples of how parents work with programs to understand policies and reach compromises that work better for them and their children.

A Compromise on Toys from Home

Manijeh loved her stuffed kitten. She slept with it at night, and holding it helped her accept leaving the house in the morning. The provider, Barbara, was adamant that children not bring toys from home, but Manijeh's mother, Nyazi, decided to ignore the policy. Nyazi felt bad about needing to herd Manijeh out the door so early, and if having her stuffed kitten made it easier, then so be it.

Barbara was annoyed that Nyazi seemed to think she was above the rules. If she got to break the rules, then other parents would want to break them too. After all, there was a reason for the rule. The kids always seemed to end up fighting over special toys, someone would end up in tears, and everyone would get distracted from the planned activities. Still, Barbara ignored the infraction for a few days. Then one day, several children ended up in tears when they all wanted turns with Manijeh's kitten. And Manijeh ended up in tears when one of the children pulled the kitten out of her arms.

That day, as the children napped, Barbara called Nyazi at her job. "You know we have a policy that the kids can't bring their toys from home. I've been reluctant to say anything, but the stuffed kitten is really getting to be a problem."

Nyazi felt herself getting tense. "But you don't understand how important that kitten is to her. It makes all the difference in getting her to go in the morning."

Barbara shot back, "What if the kitten gets lost or damaged? How's she going to feel then?"

"I'm willing to take that risk. It's so important to her."

"You don't understand how much havoc it's creating here."

Nyazi was startled. It hadn't occurred to her that Manijeh's kitten could actually be causing problems at child care. She took a deep breath and decided she needed to step back for a moment. "I'm sorry. I don't want to ignore your policy. But I also want what's best for my daughter. Is there a time we could sit down and talk about this?" Nyazi's shift in attitude helped Barbara take a step back as well, and the women agreed on a time when they could talk without the children around.

As Barbara told Nyazi stories about how difficult the kitten was making things, Nyazi gained an appreciation of the policy. As Nyazi talked about how attached Manijeh was to the kitten and how desperately she wanted to bring it, Barbara gained an appreciation of Nyazi's dilemma. They decided that Manijeh could continue to bring her special kitten, but that she'd leave it in her cubby once she arrived. As both women worked to understand the perspective of the other, they were able to find a solution. The policy was made for important reasons, but the provider was also willing to be flexible as they looked for ways to help Manijeh adjust.

Bringing toys from home can be more complicated than it appears to be. Providers may worry that the toys will get lost or damaged and don't want to take on the responsibility of guarding a special toy in an already busy day. Special toys from home can cause disruption as other children want to play with them. Young children are often understandably possessive of their special things, and fights may erupt.

On the other hand, bringing special toys from home can help children make the transition to a new environment. The toy can provide a sense of continuity and security. Or a child may be excited about a present and want to show it off to the other children.

A provider or program that has a no-toys-from-home policy may be willing to make some compromises. There is the solution Nyazi and her provider found: leaving the toy in the child's cubby. Or the child might be allowed to show the toy during circle time. Nyazi might have experimented with allowing Manijeh to bring the kitten with her in the morning but leave it in the car when she went into child care. The provider or the parent might buy a toy similar to the child's own so it's available to her at child care. Barbara eventually picked up a couple of stuffed kittens similar to Nyazi's and added them to the basket of stuffed animals that all the children played with.

Understanding Illness and Head Lice Policies

When Carol arrived to pick up Jimmy from child care, she found a note in his cubby: "Your child has been exposed to head lice. Please check carefully to see that he has not been infested." The note went on to explain that, if head lice were found, the child's hair should be washed with a special shampoo, all bedding should be washed, and carpets should be well vacuumed.

The first thing Carol did when she got Jimmy's seat belt fastened was to check his head for nits. And there they were. Carol sighed. She knew she had a lot of work ahead of her. When she got home she started right in stripping beds. After she got Jimmy shampooed and the carpets vacuumed, she called her neighbor Terese, whose child had been over to play with Jimmy yesterday. She felt humiliated telling Terese that her child may have gotten head lice from Jimmy.

"How clean is that place you take Jimmy?" Terese asked.

"It looks clean to me," Carol answered.

"Maybe it's some of the other families. Do they keep their kids clean?"

Now, in addition to feeling humiliated, Carol was worried. Had she put her son in a child care with dirty families? Why did they let children attend when they had head lice anyway? Carole decided she needed to know more about this problem.

After she got Jimmy to bed, she looked up head lice on the Internet. She learned that head lice are extremely common, that having lice is not a sign of dirty families, and that having lice occurs at all socioeconomic levels. She also learned that it's more common in public schools than in child care settings, so it was likely that one of the children in the center had gotten it from an older brother or sister.

In short, she learned that it was not through a failing at child care that her son had gotten head lice. She realized that the program had a challenging job and they'd reacted appropriately. They notified the parents, they asked parents to treat their children if they found lice, and they instituted a head check every day as the children came in. The American Academy of Pediatrics used to recommend sending a child home immediately if head lice were found. But they've changed that guideline, because once head lice have been found it's too late; exposure already has occurred. They do suggest, however, that the child not be returned to child care for a certain amount of time after the initial treatment. Providers have different policies on when infected children are to be removed and when they can return during treatment, so be sure to talk with your provider to confirm what her policy is on head lice.

It makes sense that parents wouldn't want their children exposed to any kind of infectious conditions at child care. Curious as it sounds, however, exposure to some illnesses may not be a bad thing. There is evidence that early exposure to common illnesses builds children's immunities and they miss less school later on if they've been in child care. In other words, a child can get some common childhood illnesses out of the way early rather than missing school later, when it's more apt to interfere with learning.

Be aware, however, that recurring ear infections can delay language development. If you have an infant or toddler who constantly develops ear infections as a result of repeated exposure to colds and viruses, you may want to look for a setting with fewer children.

Special circumstances can require extra vigilance. For instance, one center was caring for a child who'd gone through chemotherapy and was especially vulnerable to viruses for a time. The child's parents wrote a letter that was distributed to other families. The letter asked that families call them at home if their child had been exposed to something that, although not serious for a healthy child, would place a child with a compromised immune system in jeopardy. The other parents were happy to comply and also tended to be more cautious about sending a sick child to school. If you have any kind of special circumstance, you'll probably find that your child care provider or center is happy to work with you.

If your provider hasn't handed out a copy of her or her center's illness policies, ask her what they are and if she has them written down for you to keep for future reference. If she has no written-down policies, clarify what her policies are and write them down yourself so you can refer to them should differences of interpretation arise in the future. Contention can easily arise when it comes to making judgment calls about whether your child has an allergy or a cold or even the flu. (You can't, after all, get a written note from your doctor every time your child gets the sniffles.) The same difficulty arises over deciding when a child who has been ill is no longer infectious and can return to child care. Keeping a child home can mean missing work, which most parents can't afford to do very often. On the other hand, providers have to protect all the children in their care and need to do everything possible to prevent illnesses from spreading. Ongoing open communication and trust between you and your provider regarding these issues will save both of you a lot of misunderstanding and grief.

Changing the Sugar-Free Child Care Policy

Matt was about to celebrate his third birthday, the first one he'd be celebrating in child care. His mother, Laurie, was excited that he could share this birthday at his preschool, especially since his birthdays had always been limited to family celebrations before. She started planning his family party about a month ahead of time, and at the same time mentioned to his teacher that she planned to bring a cake for all the children to share at school.

"I'm sorry," the teacher answered. "We have a no-sugar policy here. But you could bring some fruit and crackers in honor of his birthday."

Laurie was shocked and then dismayed. This celebration was so important; she knew Matt was looking forward to sharing his cake at school. That evening she called her older sister. Linda's three children were now in elementary and high school and she'd know what to do. Linda's advice was precise: "Compromises can be made. Policies can be changed."

Some policies are in place because of legal requirements. But all policies are not written in stone. If a policy contradicts what you think is in the best interest of your child, you may be successful in making some changes. Centers and providers generally are sensitive to the needs and wishes of the parents, and a change may be made if the families want it. Some centers build into their programs formal processes to allow for family input into policies; these may range from advisory committees of parents to a suggestion box. Even if a program has no such formal process, you can still take the initiative to raise questions and make suggestions. Just keep in mind that a change in policy has to be something that serves all the families.

Laurie approached Matt's teacher. "I understand that parents don't want their kids eating sugar all the time at school, but this is a big deal for Matt. He's so looking forward to it. If the parents are okay with it, would the school let me bring a cake?"

The teacher said she didn't think the school would be all right with it, but she'd be happy to check it out with the director. "No one's questioned our no-sugar policy before," said the director. "Let's see how the parents feel about sweet treats on special occasions."

Laurie agreed to contact the parents. She called all the families in her child's room. Some were excited about the idea of the children being allowed to bring cakes on their birthdays. Others were hesitant about introducing sugar. Laurie then suggested that sugar could be limited, perhaps by having individual cupcakes so the treat would have a built-in limit. With that modification, all the parents agreed. When she reported the results to the director, the director said, "Okay, let's go with it. From now on, kids can bring cupcakes on their birthdays to share with everybody." Another compromise might have been for Laurie to bring diabetic cupcakes, which are sugar free.

The Party Dress

Nadia dropped Tasha off at child care in a pink taffeta dress with a lacy collar. "I know the kids aren't supposed to wear clothes they can't get dirty," she told her provider, "but Tasha got this from her grandma and Grandma's coming with me to pick her up today. Just make sure she wears a smock if she's going to do anything that'll get the dress dirty. Okay?"

Three hours later Nadia returned with her mother-in-law. Tasha's beautiful pink dress had a red stain on the collar and shoulder. Tasha's grandmother looked at the dress, looked at Nadia, and raised her eyebrows. "That dress wasn't cheap," was all she said.

Nadia turned to the teacher. "I asked you to put her in a smock. Did you see what happened to her dress?"

"We use washable paint," the teacher protested.

"Right. I know how well that washable paint comes out."

"Look," the teacher said. "I tried. But I bent over to help Willie tie his shoe, and by the time I stood up Tasha had already grabbed the paints. That's why we ask that children wear clothes that can get messy."

On the way to the car, Nadia's mother-in-law said, "Maybe I shouldn't buy such nice clothes anymore."

"No, it's not that," Nadia said. "Maybe I shouldn't put her in her nice clothes when she goes to child care." Nadia explained to her mother-in-law that she'd wanted her to see how lovely Tasha looked in the new dress she'd given her. But her timing wasn't right. "I can't expect her to get into her school activities and not get dirty."

As fun as it is to show off new clothing, remember that teachers and child care providers are focused on helping your child develop independence and enthusiasm for activities. A child cannot enter into painting a picture or climbing in the playground or making clay figures with unfettered curiosity and creativity if she needs to worry about keeping her clothes clean.

Doing the Best He Could with a Traffic Jam

Paulo got a call just as he was leaving work, a call he'd been waiting for all day. He knew he had to take the extra ten minutes and get his questions answered while he had the other person on the line. As a result, he had to race to his car and push the speed limit on his way to pick up Eduardo. This had been a problem between him and the provider when he first started taking Paulo to Michelle's house. She'd explained to him that she had to leave her house at exactly 5:30 PM in order to pick up her elderly mother from an adult day care program. If she didn't get there on time, she had to pay extra. So Paulo was well aware of being on time.

When he was about fifteen minutes away, he ran into a horrendous traffic jam. There'd been a four-car pileup on the freeway, and traffic had come to a complete stop. The first thing he felt was panic. Then he pulled out his cell phone and called. "I'm so sorry, Michelle. I'll be there as soon as I possibly can."

Michelle understood that Paulo was trapped. She put Eduardo on the phone so his father could reassure him that he'd be there soon. When Paulo arrived ten minutes late, he asked Michelle what the late fee was. "It's okay. I know you were stuck in traffic, and there was nothing you could do," she replied.

But Paulo insisted on paying her. "You're going to have to pay your mother's late fee, and I should cover that, so please tell me what it is." Eduardo started begging his father to look at a picture he'd drawn. Paulo told Eduardo he'd look at the picture in the car, because Michelle had to leave right away to pick up her mother.

Policies concerning drop-off and pick-up times are established for good reasons and are generally strict. It's very helpful if parents understand this and make a point of being on time. If you find you simply cannot avoid being late, call, apologize, and offer to compensate the provider for her time.

Children may also drag their feet when it's time to leave. "I need a drink of water" or "Look at what I did today" can cause further delays. You may want to please your child, but unless it's really important—he's going to wet his pants if he doesn't go to the bathroom immediately—be prompt in leaving, especially if you arrived late.

Nondiscriminatory Hiring

Diane was attending the parent open house at the Twin Pines Preschool Center in early October. The director, Carla, was telling Diane about the student interns they'd have this year. Each semester, Twin Pines took three interns from a nearby graduate program in early child development. Diane was glad there'd be an extra teacher in her daughter's room. When Carla started telling Diane about Joe, the intern who'd be in her daughter's room, Diane was surprised.

"A man?" she asked, frowning. The first place her thoughts went was to a news story last spring about a child molester in a town about fifty miles north of them. She knew child molesters were usually men.

Carla seemed flustered. "He's a very nice young man, at the top of his class, and he really seems to have a gift with children."

Diane had heard of pedophiles getting jobs where they'd have access to children. Joe might be just fine, but Diane wasn't taking any chances with her daughter. "I'm sure he is," she said to Carla, "but I may switch my daughter to another class."

There is heightened consciousness of child sexual

abuse in today's world, and highly publicized stories of abuse in child care settings have left parents even more worried. Just as people can feel the symptoms of a highly publicized illness just by hearing about the illness, they can become hypervigilant about abuse if they've been reading stories about child molesters. Simply having a male working in a child care center can be enough to make some parents nervous. A generation ago it was less common for men to be involved in the care of children, and to some people, it still seems unnatural. This, combined with today's heightened awareness of sexual abuse, contributes to the fear some people have about men they don't know well caring for young children.

Carla, of course, had more information than Diane did about the issue of men working as child care providers. She knew that more men are going into the field and that it benefits children. Children love getting attention from males as well as females. Male teachers and providers give children a role model that broadens their way of looking at the world and at what men and women can do. Carla also knew that sexual abuse in child care settings is extremely rare, and there's no reason to expect that a man working in child care has intentions different from those of a woman working in child care. Carla also knew that uninformed prejudice keeps people from appreciating the presence of men in a child care setting.

She was puzzled about how to explain all this to Diane. Carla understood that it's hard to leave your child with someone you don't know, particularly if you have suspicions about that person. She told Diane that she understood her fear, and that all the publicity about sexual abuse made it a very frightening prospect.

As Diane began to feel she was being listened to, she was able to listen to Carla in turn. Carla talked with her about how she shared Diane's concern that the children would be safe at the center. She explained that they did careful background checks of new employees. She also explained some things Diane didn't know about child sexual abuse. She said, "Abuse is extremely rare in child care settings. A child is actually more apt to be touched inappropriately by an adult they know, a relative, or a friend." Diane frowned. Carla continued, "A lot of parents are surprised to hear that. Now I don't mean to suggest you shouldn't be alert to this problem in child care. It can happen, and there are specific signs you should be aware of."

When Diane began to feel that Carla was watching out for her child, she rethought the idea of moving her daughter. Over the next month Diane got to know Joe better, and she became as excited about his being in the program as Carla was.

Child care programs are required to follow nondiscriminatory hiring policies. They can be sued if they refuse to hire people because of their gender, age, religion, or race. Fears can arise for parents who have learned to associate certain attributes with, for instance, gender or age. Such fears, however, are often based on erroneous information or even prejudices that have become so ingrained that a person isn't aware of their presence. Concern for our children's welfare can bring to the surface deep prejudices we hardly know we have. It's important to notice prejudices and not let them keep our children from benefiting from the rich experiences they can have with many different people. It's also important to notice our unrecognized and irrational prejudices so we don't pass them on to our children.

Sexual abuse is one of the fears people tend to associate with males. It is true that sexual abuse against children is perpetrated more often by men than by women. But it is also true that very few men sexually abuse children, and it makes no more sense to think a male teacher is going to abuse your child than it does to think a female teacher is going to teach your son to be a wimp.

Moreover, child sexual abuse is a rare phenomenon in child care settings. Nevertheless, sexual abuse is serious wherever or whenever it occurs, and if you have a concern it should be taken seriously. Some signs that you may need to explore the issue further include, but are not limited to, the following:

- experiencing pain or soreness in the genital area when walking, sitting, urinating, or defecating
- demonstrating adultlike sexual behavior
- being fearful of adults or certain individuals
- becoming extremely fearful of particular places or situations
- talking about or drawing sexually advanced information or behavior

Sexual abuse is far from common, and sometimes people are too quick to assume sexual abuse has occurred. Try not to panic or jump to conclusions. Still, if you see a pattern of behaviors and your concerns persist, it's important that you take action. You can report your concerns to law enforcement or child protection services, and they can help you decide if there is adequate evidence to indicate abuse. You can also take your child for an assessment by a mental health professional who specializes in treating child sexual abuse.

• • •

Points to Remember and Discuss

- Policies, written or unwritten, are generally established to make things work better for everybody.

- You need to know what a provider's policies are before you enroll your child. If something about a policy is getting in the way for your family and your child, or if something about a policy is puzzling to you, talk to your provider.

- You need to advocate for yourself. At the same time, try to understand the policy from the provider's perspective as well. Providers have to think about the needs of all the children and families, which is a point of view different from yours.

- You can do research on guidelines, rules, and regulations in your state that affect a given policy, and you can talk with parents with children in different settings to compare policies.

- Sexual abuse in child care settings with male staff (or family members in home settings) is extremely rare and unlikely. If you have concerns about abuse, discuss them with your provider and get clarification on her hiring policies.

Values

Chapter 5
Finding Common Values between Home and Child Care

One important job of parents is to teach their children values. Especially during the crucial years from birth to age five or six, the parents or principal caretakers are a child's most important teachers. They are the persons who have the most profound influence on a child's moral development. What you do and what you say creates the foundation upon which your child forms his values. You and the other primary caretaker(s) in your home are the first people your child will look to for guidance about what's right and what's wrong. He will absorb your values like water absorbs salt.

Of course, teachers, friends, and community will also have an impact on your child's values, and more so as he gets older. Because parents usually want their children's environment to reinforce the values they teach, you'll probably look for a child care setting where values seem similar to yours. This doesn't mean there should be no differences between home and child care. Differences can both inform your child about the values your family holds and broaden his perspective.

You'll find a world of differences both between and within child care settings. You may find different kinds of families—blended families, families with single parents, families of races different from yours, families with different sexual orientations, families in which grandparents are raising grandchildren.

Exposure to such differences can be a rich experience; it can also feel threatening. Sometimes parents fear that exposure to a family that holds values different from their own might change their child's values. In fact, the opposite tends to be true. Broad exposure to difference provides parents opportunities for conversations with their child that cement their own values. What generally happens is that the values that define your family become much clearer to your child. This, he thinks, is not what my family does; this is what my family does. You can be confident that you are your child's most powerful teacher.

Gaining Clarity about Your Own Values

Values become so ingrained in us that we hardly realize they're there. As a result, we're sometimes startled when someone else behaves quite differently or sees something in a very different way. We may be surprised that a person could look at something that way, or surprised to discover that it bothers us. It can be helpful, as you begin your child care search, to think deliberately about your values, to become aware of how different values—such as the ones discussed on the following pages—might be challenged or supported in a child care setting, and then to think about how important each of them is to you. Are some values so critical to you that a difference would rule out a particular child care setting? Are there some you can be flexible about? How flexible? Think about the value areas discussed below.

>Cuss Words and Other "Bad" Words

Many people don't want their young children to use the obvious cuss words. Still, children are exposed to them, at a friend's house, by older siblings, through television, sometimes even at home by the very people who most want children not to say them—their parents. You can count on most child care settings to discourage children from using these words.

Societal standards change with the times, however, and there can be a lot of latitude in which words different people consider bad. Words used affectionately in some homes are seen as pejorative in others. For example, when Emma called Caitlin a "stinker" at child care, Caitlin's eyes got big. She told the provider what Emma had called her, and Emma retorted, "That's what my daddy calls me."

Even more controversial are the words for body parts that families find either acceptable or unacceptable. You might use the word "butt," while another family would object to any word except "bottom." Most parents, and certainly the great majority of child care providers, would prohibit the word "ass," even though it's now commonly used on prime-time television. And, while most early childhood professionals are comfortable using standard anatomical terms such as penis and vagina when referring to a child's privates, some families may still find using them with young children objectionable. Think about the language you use and what you can be comfortable with. Find out what's allowed at your child care setting and discuss this candidly with your provider. Let her know what your standards are and what you prefer your child not to hear or say.

> Nudity

Families can vary enormously in their attitudes toward nudity. Many child care providers allow very young children to use the toilet in front of each other, especially during toilet training. You may feel okay about this; you may not. You may or may not feel fine about young children changing clothes in front of each other. Find out whether your provider has any policies about these issues. If you're not sure how you feel, take a day to visit and pay attention to your comfort level as you experience situations firsthand.

> Getting Dirty

It's helpful if you can be clear with yourself about how important keeping your child's clothes clean is to you. Providers often focus on providing children with stimulating experiences, even if that means their clothes get dirty or stained. Also, providers may simply find it impossible to ensure that every child stays clean during the day.

The children themselves may look dirty as well. Green gunk on a nose or dried remnants of a snack on a cheek may pose no health hazard, so the provider lets them go in favor of attending to more important tasks. Or the provider focuses on helping the children learn independence and allows them to be responsible for their appearance.

Sometimes cultural differences come into play here. One culture may view keeping children clean as the job of the adults who care for them, while other cultures may place more emphasis on children's exploration or responsibility. One example of a cultural difference posing a child care challenge occurred when a Japanese family moved into a community. One of the parents' hygiene habits was to wash their children's feet before meals. They were shocked when this wasn't done at their children's new child care. These parents and the provider were able to compromise so that the family's Japanese tradition could be honored in this new setting. The family supplied baby wipes for their children to wash their feet before meals, and the provider made sure that this was done.

>Physical Contact

A program may have rules governing physical contact that seem too restrictive for your children to feel at home. You may even feel that your child isn't getting enough nurturing and comforting. For example, if you do a lot of hugging and cuddling in your home, a program in which children aren't allowed to kiss adults or each other or aren't allowed to sit on adults' laps may feel cold to you. Or you may not like other adults touching your child too much and your program permits contact that is more demonstrative than you prefer. Either of these extremes often can be taken care of with a simple non-critical statement of your concerns and wishes. You might say something like "I want you to feel free to hold and hug my child as much as you feel she needs it. We hug a lot at home and I think showing affection is important." Or you might feel the need to say something like "I don't mean this personally, but I'd rather our son not get held so much and that you comfort and praise him more with words rather than with hugs and kisses. Independence is an important value for us, and we want him to learn to handle things on his own and not expect adults to take care of him every time he's upset."

>Responding to Aggression

Some people teach their children never to hit under any circumstances. Those at the other end of the continuum tell their child, "If someone hits you, hit them back. You've got a right to defend yourself." Acceptable responses to aggression are often culturally influenced. Be aware that it is part of most school cultures to teach children not to be aggressive or hit back. You should be able to expect a program to teach your child how to be safe, but you'll want to understand the methods they employ.

>Competition

Some parents value competition. They believe it promotes excellence and they want their children challenged by the achievements of others. They like to have their children participate in competitive games. Other parents value cooperation over competition and want to down-play competitive games in favor of team-building efforts. Parents somewhere in the middle value cooperation but appreciate a bit of competition as a healthy means of challenging children to excel.

>Respect for Elders

Although respect is a value common to most everyone, how we choose to show it may vary. Some people expect their children to address elders by their last names—Mrs. Johnson, for instance, or Mr. Kaplan. Others may feel that first names are okay in a casual situation or when a relationship is informal but encourage their kids to use titles and last names with adults in authority. Still others are comfortable with, or even prefer, children being allowed to address everyone by first names. They see this as an acknowledgment that a child has as much value as an adult. Find out whether expectations in child care settings you consider match yours.

Developing Shared Understandings

>Differing Perspectives

Even though a child care program or provider may hold values similar to yours, there may be differences in the way values are expressed and there may be families in the program whose values are quite different from yours. Keep in mind that your primary focus should be the values your child is learning. It is the provider who must be concerned about meeting the needs of all the families, including families that are different from yours. Understanding from both sides will be required when families express values differently.

Consider this example. A preschool located in a nature center attracts both parents who are hunters and parents who are vegetarians. Two particular families were attracted to the center because of their interest in animals, but their attitudes toward animals differ. The teacher, Ben, was able to help both families feel comfortable when he encouraged the children to share their differences, and a lively discussion resulted. It was important for the staff to both honor the values of the two families and clearly support each family's home values. The most important value being reinforced here was "That's what you do in your family."

A common experience of value differences arises around holidays, and holiday traditions provide a rich opportunity for discussion and learning. Different faiths celebrate different holidays, and programs may honor this by celebrating representative holidays from many faiths. This is something you can discuss with the provider. If you feel that your family's cultural or religious holidays are being ignored, raise the issue. If you firmly believe that your children should celebrate or witness only the holidays of your faith, you may need to find a specific kind of child care program. Similarly, different religious traditions may cause discomfort. If you're considering a family child care home where grace is always said before meals and this contradicts your religious perspective, you may wish to find a different place. The same is true if grace is not part of the tradition at a child care setting and it's important to you that your child says grace before every meal.

Talking about Different Values

While a provider may hold some values that are different from yours, you should be able to work together if those differences are not extreme. And although you can't expect a provider to have exactly the same values you have, you can expect her to be respectful of your values. Similarly, you'll need to be respectful of the values of others in the program.

You may be able to ask for some accommodations, but not for changes that are so dramatic a program would cease to meet other families' expectations if a provider agreed to them. For example, if your family is vegetarian, other families might not mind if the provider eliminated red meat from the lunch menu to accommodate your child. But they'd no doubt be upset if the provider switched to an all-vegetarian menu. Again, you'd need to search for a compromise.

Talking about differences in values can help your child learn to be respectful while also reinforcing your family's values. What, for instance, do you say if Sally tells Carl that killing animals is bad, and Carl's father is a hunter? What if Ali tells Sunny her daddy is a girl because he wears a ponytail? Ask your provider how she handles these kinds of issues. The two of you can work toward giving your child the same message about values.

If Sunny or Ali were your child, for example, you might talk about how lots of people think boys should

always have short hair, but some boys and men wear
their hair long. You could talk about how fashions differ
in different countries and in different cultures and read a
children's picture book that illustrates this. If Sally or
Carl were your child, you might talk about how people
have different beliefs about what is okay. The way your
family feels about hunting is different from how the other family feels. Families do things in different ways.
You'd then want to talk with the provider to see if her
approach reflects the values you want taught.

> Why All Those Nosy Questions?

Child care programs may delve into your life in a way
that surprises you. Some programs require a lot of pre-
enrollment paperwork. Head Start is required to do
home visits with the children enrolled in their programs.
Other programs may ask questions about a parent's high-
est level of education, who else lives in the home,
whether the child has been enrolled in other programs,
and so on.

Being asked for all this personal information may feel
intrusive to you. Or you may be worried that you have to
answer every question correctly or your child won't be
accepted. Keep in mind that generally these questions are
asked because the provider wants to understand your
child as well as she possibly can so she can better meet
your child's needs.

For instance, if a provider knows your child has had
little experience being away from home, she won't be surprised if it takes your child a bit longer to adjust to child
care. If she knows your child has older school-age sib-

lings, she'll be prepared for the possibility of inappropriate language. If your child says, "Jack took me to the circus," she'll be more apt to know who Jack is and be able to respond in a way that keeps the conversation going. If your child has had a traumatic experience with a dog, the provider will know she has to talk to you and do a lot of preparation with your child before she can bring a dog into the classroom. The more the provider knows about your child and his family, the better care she can provide.

• • •

Points to Remember and Discuss

- Teaching values is your right and your obligation as a parent: You are your child's most powerful teacher.

- The child care setting you choose can reinforce your values, it can provide a different perspective that broadens your values, or it can encourage behaviors or attitudes that conflict with your values.

- You need to take time to think about what values you want to find in your child care setting and how critical each of those values is to you.

- Differences can provide an opportunity to teach your child more about your own values and to respect the values of others.

- Your provider has to be aware of meeting the needs of all the families in the program.

- When the provider's values and your values come into conflict, you need to make the effort to find creative solutions together.

Chapter 6
Addressing Value Dilemmas

Values are an emotion-laden topic. Many people think of
values as something on which you simply cannot compromise. And this is certainly true of some values. Most
people would agree that not purposefully hurting innocent people is a rock-bottom value that you wouldn't
alter to please somebody else. But there's a host of values
that aren't so clear-cut and that offer a lot of room for
compromise. And there are also many values that people
hold in common but express in different ways. Again,
this is an area ripe for compromise.

Holidaze

It was the first night of Hanukkah. But as Rachel got
out the menorah, all David could talk about was
Christmas. He attended child care in Mary's home four
days a week. Rachel knew when she started David there
that Mary would celebrate Christmas with the children.
They'd talked about it even, and Rachel had told Mary
that would be fine. She was used to being surrounded by

Christmas. How could it be otherwise in America? But this was getting more intense than she'd anticipated.

David had been aglow with excitement the day the children put up the Christmas tree. "I made a silver star for the tree, Mommy!" Next he began singing Christmas carols. "Away in a Manger" was suddenly his favorite song. And now, on the first night of Hanukkah—a time that felt to Rachel like an oasis for her family—all David cared about was Christmas and Santa Claus. Rachel felt like crying. How was she supposed to teach him to cherish his Jewish heritage when all he heard four days a week was Christmas, Christmas, Christmas? Enough was enough.

The next day she phoned Mary. "I know we talked about Christmas celebrations, but I feel like David is drowning in Christmas. How much celebrating are you doing over there, anyway?"

Mary seemed taken aback. "I told you Christmas is a big deal for me. I love it, and the kids love it too. I hope you're not asking me to give that up."

Before she said anything more, Rachel reminded herself that this holiday stuff was pretty emotional for everyone. "No, of course I don't want you to give it up. And you're right. David loves it. But I want David to love his own holidays too."

Mary had promised she would pay attention to Hanukkah, and she told Rachel that she'd read a book about Hanukkah during circle time.

"I think David needs more than that," Rachel replied. The two women brainstormed about what Mary could do to help David honor his Jewish holidays along with the Christmas holidays that were celebrated at child care. They decided that Rachel would bring a menorah to child care at lunchtime one day and tell the children about its symbolism. When David's father came to Mary's on another day, he taught the children how to play dreidel and brought them Hanukkah gelt, the foil-covered chocolate coins often handed out to children at this time. David was very excited to share his special holiday with the other children, and the others had fun learning about the Jewish holiday as well.

The friction that surfaces around holidays tends to reflect differing religious or cultural values or values regarding commercialism. Members of the majority culture may be unaware of any friction. All American children, regardless of their religion or culture, become experts on Christmas, Easter, Halloween, and Thanksgiving. But American children of minority cultures may find that many of their holidays and traditions are ignored. For instance, Rosh Hashanah and Yom Kippur are the most important holidays of the Jewish year. Yet school and work go on as if nothing important were happening, which feels strange to Jewish children. Similarly, most of American culture doesn't recognize Ramadan, an important religious observance for Muslims. There are many other examples. If your family is a member of a religion or culture whose holidays and traditions go unnoticed in child care, you may wish to talk with your provider about finding ways to change that.

Certain holidays may be especially tough for families

who believe it is wrong to celebrate them. Some fundamentalist Christian families do not want their children exposed to Halloween, which they consider a pagan holiday. Jehovah's Witnesses may not celebrate any holidays or birthdays. If holidays that you don't want your child to be part of are an integral part of your child care, a compromise may be possible. Perhaps your provider will allow your child to skip that particular day without paying for it. If it's a celebration with some flexibility, perhaps your provider can arrange the celebration for a day when your child would be absent anyway. The father of a child whose mother had died the previous year asked his child care provider to save stories and activities celebrating Mother's Day for a time when his daughter would be absent, hoping she wouldn't be as tender the following year.

Pretty Painted Fingernails

The day Mike came home from Sunnyside Child Care Center with bright painted fingernails was the day his mother, Catherine, called "the day Daddy saw red." When Mike's father, George, walked in the house and took one look at Mike's nails, his face did turn almost red. He started sputtering, and Catherine gave him a look. So he read the mail before going back into the family room, where Mike was playing.

"Hey, sport, where'd you get those nails?" he asked.
"At school," said Mike, holding up his hand proudly.
"Who painted them?"
"My teacher."

"Ooookay. How about we do a puzzle?"

George dropped Mike at preschool on his way to work each day, so the next morning he asked Mike's teacher for a word. He was feeling pretty cross, and he didn't mince words. "I don't think it's appropriate to be making my son look and act like a girl. He's at an age where he's learning values, and if we don't teach him what it means to be male, he may get confused."

At first the teacher was confused. "What do you mean?" she asked.

"Those nails. You painted his fingernails bright red yesterday. Where I come from, boys don't wear painted fingernails."

"Oh," she nodded her head. Then she explained that one of the other parents is a manicurist and had come to school the day before to talk about her job. She started painting one girl's nails to demonstrate what she does, and then all the children had wanted their nails painted.

George realized he'd jumped to conclusions about what was going on at preschool, but he still didn't like the idea of Mike parading around with red nails. The teacher explained to him that at Mike's age, having painted nails was essentially like playing dress-up or putting on clown makeup. It was playacting. She also told George that if she'd told Mike he couldn't have his nails painted when all the other children were doing it, he wouldn't have understood. He would have felt left out. Now that George, too, understood, he felt much calmer. He chuckled. "Maybe a little warning would have helped," he said. "Maybe next time you can paint his nose and cheeks red, too, so he can be a real clown."

"He'd probably like that," she laughed.

Parents are sometimes taken aback when their boys get painted nails, dress up in girls' clothing, or do other typically feminine things. But for young children it's all part of trying out a lot of identities. Little boys love to play dress-up as much as little girls do. Young children are often attracted to bright colors and to clothes and accessories that glitter and shine or that look unique. A little boy's choice to play dress-up in clothing or accessories that happen to be feminine means absolutely nothing about his gender identity.

It's helpful to understand that dressing up in girls' clothing will not influence your child's understanding of his gender. You could also ask your provider to offer dress-up clothes that are gender neutral, giving boys an opportunity to choose fun, glittery clothing that isn't identifiable as girls' clothing.

The National Association for the Education of Young Children (NAEYC) offers guidance to providers in finding, along with parents, solutions to difficult situations. NAEYC suggests providers should listen closely and respectfully to the parents, consider the effect on the child, and accommodate the parents' request as long as it does not jeopardize the child's well-being.

Television

Fatuma put on some music to listen to while she cleaned the house. As soon as Naja heard the music, she started dancing, a very particular kind of dance, and not a kind

Fatuma had ever seen in her house. Naja's moves were provocative, and Fatuma didn't like it. "Where did you learn to dance like that?" she asked her daughter.

"At Phyllis's house," said Naja. "From the television."

"How often do you watch television?" Fatuma asked her four-year-old.

"Every day."

Fatuma was upset. She and her husband, Yusuf, had talked with Phyllis about television. She'd told them the children in her family child care hardly ever watched television. Fatuma and Yusuf liked the sound of that compared to some places they'd visited, but even so, they preferred that Naja did not watch any television without their supervision. If their daughter was going to watch television, they wanted to be in charge of which programs she saw. They asked Phyllis if she would give Naja a different activity to do in the kitchen during those "hardly ever" times the other children were watching television. Now it looked to Fatuma as if "hardly ever" meant "always" and that Naja wasn't doing something more wholesome in the kitchen while the TV was on.

That weekend Fatuma called Phyllis to find out what was going on. Phyllis explained that she put a video on for the older children to watch while the younger ones napped. Sometimes they watched a couple of half-hour cartoon shows.

"That doesn't sound like hardly ever to me," said Fatuma.

"It's only an hour a day," protested Phyllis.

"I guess we had different ideas about what hardly ever meant."

Phyllis also explained to Fatuma that she did take out art materials for Naja and arrange them on the kitchen table, but it was almost impossible to keep her away when the others were watching a video. Naja kept running in to see the video, and she felt awful about nagging her back into the kitchen all the time when Naja obviously wanted to be part of the group. Still, she did keep after her. She didn't let her watch with the other children, but there were times when she did see a video for a while.

Some parents have strong feelings about their children watching either very limited television or no television at all, while others allow a lot of television viewing. Some parents feel the media have more influence over children's values than they're comfortable with, and they want to be in control of transmitting values. They may resent the commercialism and hate it when their children come home begging for toys marketed on cartoon shows. This is an important issue to think about as you select a child care setting. If your child already goes to a family child care where television is part of the day, it may be an issue to revisit with your provider if you haven't talked about it lately.

Television tends to be more of an issue in family child care settings than in centers. Some parents choose family child care because they appreciate the homelike atmosphere—eating at a kitchen table, playing in a living room or backyard, and playing with children of various ages.

They like the idea of a relaxed environment. For many of these parents, it will seem normal for the children to watch some TV during the day, just as they might at home. Others don't see television as part of their home environment, or they expect television viewing to be limited to an occasional educational video.

If this is an important issue for you, you may want to be very specific in your questioning regarding television. If the provider says the children watch television "occasionally" or "hardly ever," ask what that means. Once a month? Once a week? Once a day? Such terms can mean different things to different people. Ask, too, for specific information on which shows the children watch. Can children bring in videos to share? Are there rules about what kinds of videos they can watch? What network shows can the children watch? You may want to know that a responsible adult is in the room with the children when they're watching TV. If so, ask about this as well. Perhaps it's fine with you if your child watches *Mister Rogers' Neighborhood* every morning, but you wouldn't want him to watch an action show such as *Power Rangers*. Perhaps you think a show like *Power Rangers* is fun; all the other children watch it and they all play Power Ranger games, and you want your child to be part of it. Think about what you're comfortable with and then ask very specific questions.

Fatuma and Yusuf did not want their child watching any television, and both they and their provider thought offering an alternative activity to Naja would work out. But Phyllis soon found it wasn't that easy. Once she realized that Naja felt left out, she started trying to talk the other children out of watching the video they'd come to expect during afternoon quiet time. Then she started to resent the change in the comfortable routine she'd established before Naja joined them.

It's important to realize that it isn't reasonable to expect your child to do a separate activity in a different room when the rest of the group is doing something he would like to be part of. Your child is apt to feel left out and either constantly press to be part of the action or passively accept something that makes him feel bad.

Both her parents and her provider wondered if Naja was going to have to be moved to another setting, but none of them really wanted that to happen. In every other way, Naja's parents were happy with the care Phyllis provided. And Phyllis was very fond of Naja and hated to lose her. Ultimately they were able to work out a compromise. They agreed that Phyllis would provide the children only with videos, not with television programs and the commercials that accompany them, and Naja's parents were able to look at a list of the videos so they could feel comfortable with the values being portrayed. They also agreed to contribute toward the extra rental fees and costs of purchasing some videos.

• • •

Points to Remember and Discuss

- You may experience friction over how your child care setting is influencing the values your child is forming.

- Some conflicts arise from misunderstandings that can be resolved with a direct inquiry and discussion; others arise over practices and behaviors that compromise values important to you.

- You can identify the issues important to you—for example, religious holidays and practices, gender roles, and what kinds of television shows are allowed in your setting—and then schedule a meeting to discuss them with your provider.

- By talking with your provider with an open mind, you usually can find respectful ways to both accommodate each other's perspective and help your child understand and respect differences while you reinforce your own values.

- Only you can decide if a values issue is important and non-negotiable enough to warrant looking for a child care setting that is more compatible with your values.

Child Development Issues

Chapter 7
Stages of Development

Childrearing practices sometimes seem to go through fads, and to some extent this is true. Nevertheless, considerable research has been done on how children learn and on the stages children go through as they grow. Such research can help us make informed judgments about certain childrearing practices. For example, doctors once thought that infants should be fed on a certain schedule. Mothers were told to nurse their babies every four hours. But research has shown that babies become hungry more frequently than every four hours and that they benefit from being fed when they're hungry. Understanding the stages of development children go through helps parents and providers alike tailor their teaching and guidance to a child's needs.

Although knowledge about child development is valuable in guiding our childrearing practices, it's important to remember that every child's development is unique. For instance, it's common for two-year-olds to be working on what's called the developmental task of autonomy—of understanding that they are separate human beings. One of the ways they do this is by saying "no" to virtually anything and everything. But every two-year-old isn't alike. Some children enter this stage earlier than others, or later. Similarly, every three-year-old isn't exactly the same, and so on through the ages and stages of development. Family life, culture, experience, innate qualities such as genetic predispositions, and other factors all affect development. The point is that, though they may not look alike as they do it or enter each stage at the same time, all children do tend to go through a certain, predictable sequence of development.

Developmentally Appropriate Programming

Some parents look at their child's preschool or day care and wonder why their child doesn't get more instruction in reading and writing. Some are comparing their child's experience with that of children in other programs or with their own experience. What they're usually remembering, however, is their experience in elementary school, not in preschool or child care settings. Preschools and many child care centers are organized around active learning and developmentally designed play environments rather than having children sit at desks and be led through the linear learning activities a child might do at a later developmental stage.

You're likely to find less formal curriculum and structure in a family child care setting, which tends to function more like a home, with less formal expectations about what children will be doing at a given time. Still, many family child care settings, especially those with a provider who goes through regular training to maintain her license, also create an atmosphere for learning that is based on the same knowledge that provides the foundation for preschool programs and child care centers.

>Discovery-Based Learning

Parents are often concerned that their child won't be ready for kindergarten and first grade if she isn't being drilled in numbers and shapes and letters. What's actually more important, however, is that a child be able to express herself, to control her impulses, to remember things on purpose, and to think about alternatives. The idea is that, to be ready for school, children need to know how to learn. They have to have built good habits of the mind, such as having a disposition toward being a reader or a risk taker, toward being curious and interested. There is strong research support for curriculum that focuses on children making choices and participating in activities that help them discover things for themselves.

Most preschools and centers today use this participation-based approach to teaching, in which much of the learning takes place within carefully designed and programmed play and activity environments. You'll also find some preschools and centers with programs that are modeled on a particular philosophy. Four such program models are briefly described below.

Montessori Programs

Maria Montessori was a pediatrician who developed an early childhood education approach that encourages children to learn through direct sensory experience. Her model included developing play materials to teach concepts, designing ways for teachers to demonstrate proper use of these materials, and creation of a child-appropriate environment, for example, child-size furniture, for learning. Teachers are expected to have training specific to the philosophy.

Even without knowing Maria Montessori's name, most of us are familiar with Montessori materials, which have become prototypes for many of the better designed toys for young children. For instance, many homes and child care settings have a stacking toy, a small plastic pole on which graduated rings are stacked from largest to smallest. This toy is an example of a typical Montessori material. The children are taught a certain way to use the materials offered to them. They develop math, reading, and other skills as they progress through the materials. They also are taught to care for the materials in a specific way.

Children work individually in a Montessori program. The classrooms tend to be very quiet, neat, organized, and controlled. There is much variability in how strictly a program adheres to the Montessori philosophy, but a large number of preschools and many centers use at least some of the equipment and a lot of the pedagogical ideas.

Waldorf Programs
Waldorf programs are based on the teachings of Rudolf Steiner, an Austrian philosopher and lecturer who emphasized protecting and nurturing the natural modes of development and interior growth all children experience. As with Montessori programs, Waldorf teachers are

expected to have training specific to the philosophy. Skills are expected to emerge naturally as children pursue their interests, and children are not overtly taught to read until seven years of age. Waldorf schools emphasize creative expression, generally use only natural materials, and tend not to have commercial toys in classrooms. These environments strive for natural settings with a fanciful, organic quality, such as including lots of plants and having tree houses for the children to play in.

Reggio Emilia

This program philosophy was developed in Reggio Emilia, a village in northern Italy, by educator Loris Malaguzzi and has been popular in the United States during the past decade. It focuses on supporting children's passions and engaging their minds in the present rather than on preparing them for future educational expectations. Children in such a program tend to work in small groups on projects of particular interest to the children, and cooperative learning is emphasized. The visual arts are stressed. There is generally an artist in residence whose only job is to provide an art studio for children. These classrooms tend to be lively and active and, although aesthetics are highly valued, there is an appreciation for the messiness inherent in creativity.

Creative Curriculum®

This program was developed by educator Diane Trister Dodge and is widely used by programs in the U.S. Department of Defense and in Head Start. It is essentially a formalization of a discovery-based program, and the curriculum can be purchased by a preschool. It emphasizes the physical environment of the classroom, with multiple interest centers. Teachers are given guidelines for creating a classroom environment and providing appropriate activities as well as strategies for facilitating children's learning.

This brief overview of some of the specific models and philosophies that have helped shape discovery-based learning can be a starting place for you to begin exploring what developmentally appropriate practices look like in successful child care settings. Keep in mind, however, that not using one of these models or not following all the practices suggested here doesn't mean that your provider isn't doing a good job. Talk with your provider about her understanding of your child's present needs in the context of his physical, emotional, social, and cognitive development. What you'll learn from such an ex-change can be a helpful gauge in deciding whether your goals for child care—beyond just having a safe and fun place for your child to be while you're at work—are being met.

If you haven't thought about what your goals are, exploring some of these models through your own research and by discussing these ideas with your provider may get you started in working together to further enrich your child care experience no matter what setting your child is in. You may find that you want a more structured, programmatic approach to reach your goals, or you may find that the personal, nurturing environment provided in a family day care setting is best for your child's ongoing learning and development. No matter what model or philosophy is being used, the most important factor is having

a caring and competent provider, whe-ther she works in a
center or a home. If you and your child trust your provider and you feel your child is getting good nurturing
along with a variety of developmentally appropriate activities in a safe, stimulating environment, then the rest will
come.

Providers as a Resource

Research on the stages of child development can also
guide childrearing practices. Research suggests that children learn new behaviors best when they are given guidance rather than punishment, when they are taught
rather than blamed. Because guidance is most effective
when it's given by a person the child loves and trusts,
building a loving, nurturing relationship with your child
is critical. Most parents know this, but putting even basic
information into practice can be confusing when parents
feel besieged by so many educational and childrearing
theories.

One of the gifts that early childhood teachers and
child care providers can give parents is information—
information about child development, information about
what to expect from a child at a given age, information
about how their child compares to others his age. Many
child care providers and teachers have taken classes, read
extensively, and attended professional development conferences. They've delved into the body of knowledge pro-
duced by the research on child development. At minimum, good providers have the valuable basic wisdom
and insight that comes from spending time with and

closely observing many children as they change and grow
from year to year and stage to stage.

As a parent, you may have done a lot of reading as
well, and you certainly know your child better than anyone else does. You may also be getting advice from a lot
of quarters: friends, in-laws, neighbors, your parents, the
latest experts on TV and in the press. No matter how
well read you are, though, childrearing practices can be
confusing. For every article bemoaning the hurried child
there is another telling you not to let your child be left
behind. And the stakes for making the wrong decision
can seem high. None of us wants to make mistakes that
will hurt our children.

The good news is that children are resilient. We all
make mistakes, but if our intentions are good and we
meet our children's basic physical needs and their innate
need for love and nurturing, they'll be all right anyway.
Still, we want to find guidance and support for our decisions, and an experienced, professional child care provider can be a wonderful resource.

If your child is in a formal child care center or preschool, it may include a lending library, newsletters, or
lectures that contain information on child development.
Take advantage of toy-lending libraries and parent-
teacher conferences. Perhaps the best source of developmental information specific to your child will be the
casual conversations you have with the teacher or provider in any child care setting your child is in. These
conversations can tell you what your child is doing and
how her behavior fits in the greater scheme of develop-

ment. If your child is in a preschool or center with a formal curriculum, you can also ask the teacher about your child's participation and progress and how that curriculum supports developmentally appropriate learning.

Matching Methods between Home and Child Care

As discussed at the beginning of this book, the relationship you have with your child care provider makes a big difference in your child's experience. A good working partnership with your provider is one of the most important partnerships you can cultivate. Your child will benefit if you and the provider work together to guide your child's behavior in ways that fit her developmental stage. The issues considered below frequently require some coordination between parents and providers.

>Discipline

Many child care settings have specific guidelines about discipline, and they sometimes are confusing to parents. For instance, one parent was surprised by the provider's response when a toddler grabbed a toy from another child. Rather than put the toddler in time-out—which is what the parent expected—the provider simply asked the toddler to give the toy back and handed her a similar toy. Sometimes parents see a child who bites or steals or lies as being naughty, whereas the provider sees such behavior as a normal part of development that will change as the child learns.

As noted above, research suggests that guiding works better than punishment when you want to teach your child new behaviors. Guiding involves nurturing and teaching a child rather than blaming him when he does something "wrong." Most teachers and providers are aware of and practice this approach, and most of today's child care centers base their programs on it.

Confusion also can arise when parents want to give their child delayed punishment for things that happen at child care. A mother might, for example, ask a teacher to tell her child that if he says a bad word she'll tell his dad and he won't be allowed to watch television at home that night. Such a delay between behavior and consequence is so great that it is unlikely to have any impact on a very young child.

Parents sometimes want providers or teachers to provide a specific consequence to their child for certain behaviors, and the teacher may decline. It's important to remember that the teacher or provider wants to be as consistent as possible with all of the children and that her focus has to be on managing an entire classroom or, in a family setting, an entire group of children.

Finally, techniques and rules will vary depending on the individuals and the types of settings involved. For instance, in a family child care, all the children may have rest time from noon to 2:00 PM, whereas in a preschool the toddlers may be required to rest while the older children play quietly in another room.

> Toilet Training

Toilet training requires considerable coordination between provider and parent. When children are ready for toilet training, it generally comes about quickly. Children usually master this task over the course of several weeks. They practice repeatedly throughout the day, every day, and consistency between the provider and home will help to smooth this transition. What you do at home will be more effective if you and your child care provider are doing similar things.

The average age a child is toilet trained falls at around two-and-a-half to three-and-a-half years for daytime dryness and between three-and-a-half and four years for nighttime dryness, although it isn't unusual for some children to be trained even later than this. Nighttime wetting is not usually considered a problem until a child is six or seven years old. Your child can be considered completely toilet trained when he can notice the urge to use the toilet, get there in time, pull down his pants, use the toilet, pull up his pants, and wash up after himself.

Your provider can be very helpful in recognizing when your child is ready to take this exciting step. In all likelihood, she's helped a lot of children through this process. This doesn't mean the provider is always right or should make the final decision, however. Such decisions are always up to the parent. Even though your provider may be able to give you valuable insight, you know your child better than anyone else does.

When you think your child is ready to use the bathroom, talk with your provider about what methods you will use and see if you can make the experience consistent. For instance, if your child is afraid of the big toilet at child care but is used to the potty-chair or toilet seat adapter you use at home, it might help him feel comfortable if you provide the same equipment for him at child care. Your provider may also have ideas that have worked for her with other children.

Be aware that you and the teacher or provider will be responding to different pressures. For instance, you'll have the challenge of helping your child use the bathroom in a restaurant, on vacation, or in other unfamiliar places, which may make consistency difficult for you. On the other hand, the provider, especially in a child care center, may have so many children to tend to that dealing with repeated accidents is very difficult. Differing pressures may require understanding and compromises. Perhaps you want your child to go directly from diapers to underpants, but your provider wants your child to wear Pull-Ups at child care until he's completely trained. Or maybe she wants to use Pull-Ups, on field trips because the number of children she's caring for makes it difficult for her to spend much time with one child in a bathroom away from the center or home. Or perhaps you want your child to wear Pull-Ups, and the provider wants your child to experience the wetness to help her learn to use the toilet. Compromises and close coordination can make this important new behavior easier for your child to learn.

>Biting, Lying, and Other Age-Specific Behaviors

Parents often get very upset when their toddler bites another child. Providers have worked with many children and often can reassure a parent about such behavior.

Young children who do not yet have the language skills to communicate when they're frustrated are more likely to bite than are older, more verbally competent children. Your child care provider can reassure you that biting doesn't mean your child is a little monster. He'll outgrow this behavior as he realizes it isn't acceptable and learns other ways to express himself.

Many parents also tend to get upset when they hear their child telling tall tales. They worry about their child's character, whether she's going to grow up to be an honest person with integrity. A child care provider can tell you that young children often don't understand the difference between fantasy and reality. A three-year-old, for instance, is apt to be at a stage in which he engages in what's called "magical thinking." Children this age often believe that if they think something, it comes true; their thinking alone can make it happen.

Refusing to share is another behavior that is both typical of young children and upsetting to parents. Before the age of three-and-a-half or four, many children do not understand the idea of sharing. They may grab toys that other children are using or simply refuse to take turns. Most child care providers recognize that this does-n't mean a child is selfish. It simply means he is not developmentally ready to share or needs help to learn this concept. A provider can help you with ideas for how to respond appropriately in ways that keep your child and others from being hurt and how to coach your child gently in the direction of sharing.

Young children behave in ways that are perfectly normal

and yet are difficult for adults to understand or accept. Adults may judge a child based on adult thinking. It's enormously helpful to understand how your child is thinking and what she's capable of doing and comprehending as you try to teach her more mature behaviors. Most providers have a lot of experience with many children, and many have specialized knowledge that can help you as you cope with what feels like difficult behavior to you.

• • •

Points to Remember and Discuss

- Children progress predictably through certain stages of development.

- Although young children do go through a fairly predictable and similar sequence in their development, different children progress through the stages at different rates.

- Most preschool programs are designed to allow a child to learn by exploring and experiencing. Home child care settings may be less formal programmatically, but the practices of providers in those settings often are rooted in a similar "discovery" philosophy.

- Children learn new behaviors best in the context of a loving, nurturing relationship and through guidance rather than punishment.

- Child care providers and teachers can be a great resource for parents. They can provide information on child development and on how a particular child fits into the greater scheme of development.

- Providers are likely to have ideas for responding in developmentally appropriate ways to challenging yet normal, age-related behaviors related to potty training, biting, lying, and turn taking.

- As you attempt to teach your child new behaviors, coordinating methods and responses with your provider is extremely valuable.

Chapter 8
Behavioral Challenges

We're enchanted by our children—and exhausted by them. They both delight us and drive us crazy. When Willie tries to tackle his dad when they're playing football, it tickles him, but when Willie pushes Jason to the ground, it's not funny. When Tiffany mimics her older brother's way of saying "You go, girl," everyone laughs. But when she turns her innocent face toward her grandmother and says, "I hope you go to hell!" Tiffany's mother is appalled and humiliated.

Children continually offer their parents surprises—some good, some bad—as they explore the world and experiment with new behaviors. They bring some of these alternately delightful and dismaying behaviors home from child care and preschool; and they take some from home into those settings. Both parent and provider find themselves challenged by a child's behavior on occasion, and they need to talk to each other. After all, time in child care and time at home are closely intertwined for a child. Life is smoother and easier for your child if you and your provider understand what his day is like in each place and you can collaborate on making his environment consistent.

Peter and His Mom Adjust to Child Care

Sharon decided to return to work part-time when Peter was twenty months old. Peter had never been in child care, and Sharon worried that the separation would be hard on both of them. In the month before she began working, she and Peter visited the child care center several times. She sat on the floor and played with him until it seemed he was comfortable with the new toys and the other children. She practiced walking out of the room and leaving him for short periods of time. She told Carl, the provider, about all of Peter's quirks and what he liked and didn't like to eat, how she put him down for a nap, and what she did when he was hard to settle. She thought she'd done everything a parent could do to prepare her child for child care.

The first day she left Peter for the morning, he cried as if his heart were broken. He clung to her, repeating one of the only words he knew: "Mama. Mama. Mama." Sharon told him over and over that she would return. "It's only for the morning," she said, although Peter, of course, didn't understand the concept of time. She tried to hand him off to Carl, only to take him back again when he stretched toward her. Finally, she turned her back and walked out, but she was devastated. She called as soon as she got to work. Carl told her Peter had settled down, but Sharon was sure she could hear him whimpering in the background.

This scene was repeated all five mornings that week. Both Carl and Sharon were feeling the strain of it. Sharon wondered if she was being a bad mom by leaving her child to go back to work. She felt guilty and nervous. She also wondered whether Carl knew how to handle babies as well as he should. Although, Carl knew it took time for babies to get used to separating from their mothers, he thought Sharon was making it harder for Peter by the way she hovered. Both adults found themselves getting tense as Monday approached.

Sure enough, Monday morning was another repeat. When Sharon picked up Peter at the end of the morning, Carl asked if they could talk that afternoon while the children napped. When he phoned Sharon, Carl said, "I know it's painful to leave your son when he's crying like that. You must worry that he's unhappy the whole time you're gone."

Sharon felt a sense of relief when Carl seemed to understand. "Oh, it's so hard. I think I'm being a monster abandoning him like that."

"I've seen so many parents go through this," Carl said. "I think the parents may have a harder time than the children."

Sharon chuckled.

"In some ways it's harder for the children who don't yet have the words to express themselves," Carl continued. "But Peter is already learning that he can count on you to come back. When he sees me start to get the other children ready for lunch, he looks at the door and says, "Mama."

"Really?" Sharon felt some hope and relief. Carl then talked with Sharon about making the good-byes brief and matter-of-fact. He told Sharon that young children can sense their parent's anxiety and the message they get is that being left there may be dangerous. If Sharon could show confidence that Peter would be fine, Peter could borrow some of that confidence. They also talked about Sharon bringing Peter's special toy car and leaving it with him. It was only another week before Peter's whimpers had turned into merely a soulful look as his mom walked away. After another week, he was waving and saying, "Bye-bye, Mama."

The initial adjustment to child care has a lot to do with a child's developmental stage. Infants do not yet have a concept of object permanence. This means that they cannot hold a picture of their parents in their minds, so when parents leave, infants grieve. As the baby bonds with the caregiver, the provider's face becomes a substitute for the parent's face and the baby feels secure. How long this bonding takes depends on how frequently and regularly the baby goes to child care and on how caring and warm the provider is.

While parents feel relief when their baby bonds with the provider, it can also be hard to see your child reach out to someone else. Although you might feel dispensable, you aren't, of course. Your baby is far more attached to you than to anyone else. And, in fact, it is his healthy attachment to you that makes it possible for him to form attachments to other people.

For toddlers, adjusting to a program mostly has to do with adjusting to the caregiver. For preschoolers, the adjustment may be mostly to the caregiver, but it may also be to the other children as well as to the activities and the environment.

Children generally resist separation from their parents for a short period of time and then stay happily at child care. Sometimes, however, it takes longer. When this happens, it requires more patience from parents and providers alike. If your child cries for four weeks straight every time you leave, you may feel irritated or worried that your child is terribly insecure. But it may have nothing to do with your child's general level of security; it may simply reflect the nature of her personality.

Providers also talk about something called the birthday party syndrome. For the first three or four weeks, the child is thrilled to go to child care, and then suddenly one day he doesn't want to stay and he cries and fights when his parent tries to leave. When this happens, parents needn't look for a precipitating event. It usually just means that the novelty of child care has worn off.

There might, on the other hand, be a precipitating event that you wouldn't necessarily connect with increased anxiety. Christopher, for example, was used to his child care home and well adjusted there. Then one morning he protested vociferously when his father left. Later, as his father and the provider talked, they realized that Christopher's display of anxiety appeared right after his grandparents had left, after a week's stay at Christopher's house. "I bet Christopher has just understood something more about the world," the provider commented. "He now realizes that sometimes people go away."

Children's ability to separate fluctuates as they grow. Separation anxiety peaks at around the age of eight months and again around the age of eighteen months.

Often around age five, children's understanding of the world and its risks grows, and they again show more separation anxiety. Increased anxiety doesn't have to mean something bad has happened or something is wrong with your child.

Besides age, a child's adjustment is influenced by factors such as the amount of exposure she's had to separation, how much time she's spent with other children, and her personality. A child who's outgoing and flexible will adjust more easily than a child who's very shy or sensitive to transitions. Separation can be especially tough for children who don't yet have much language or who speak a language different from that of the caregiver. Under such circumstances, you can expect adjusting to take a little longer.

There are things you and your provider can do to ease the adjustment for your child. Don't share your own anxiety with your child. Remember that children look to their parents for cues about safety. Make your good-byes brief. Don't hang around and spy on your child. If he notices you, his anxiety will start all over again. You can also give your child physical evidence of your presence, a photo, perhaps, or an object that smells like you. Sometimes parents sleep on the crib sheets their baby later sleeps on in child care.

You can also ask your provider if you can call in the middle of the day to see how your child is doing. Your provider can help your child write notes to you, or use a toy telephone to have pretend conversations with you. The provider might keep one of your family photo books in her classroom or home, or help your child understand in concrete terms when you'll return by saying something such as, "Daddy is coming after snacktime." Witnessing warmth and trust between you and your provider is also helpful to your child. Seeing you giving the provider a friendly touch or smiling and telling jokes with her sends the significant message that you like the provider and this is a safe place.

My Little Jesse James

Three-year-old Marty loved little cars. Every time he went into a store with his dad, he begged for a new car. He stuffed his pockets with them and pulled them out at the dinner table to drive them around his plate. He had to have at least one with him when he went to the doctor or the library or a friend's house. He'd acquired so many cars it was hard to keep track of them all.

When the preschool teacher asked Marty's dad if any new little cars had shown up in their house, Joe was startled. "I don't know that I'd recognize a new one," he replied. Laura explained that the school's Matchbox cars were disappearing, and she'd noticed Marty slipping one into his pocket at clean-up time. "Can you check his pockets when you get home just to be sure?" she asked.

Joe felt a bit funny about the request. Did Laura actually think his kid was stealing? He did what the teacher had asked but found no Matchbox car in Marty's pocket. When Joe picked up Marty the following afternoon, Laura stopped Marty as they were leaving. She checked his pocket and found a little blue car. She took it and bent down to Marty, "Honey, this car belongs to the school and you need to leave it here. Otherwise there won't be cars for you to play with when you're at school."

Joe felt embarrassed. A couple of parents who were picking up their kids at the same time saw Laura checking Marty's pockets. Joe's face turned red. They must think we're a shady family, he thought. He stewed over the incident once he got home. After Marty was in bed, he finally could tell his wife. "Laura did a pat-and-search on Marty in front of the other parents today. She practically called him a thief. He's a good kid. He just forgot the car was in his pocket, that's all. I don't know if I trust her with Marty anymore."

Marty's mother had had only good experiences with Laura and she felt confident that it was a good program for Marty. She urged Joe to give Laura a call and talk it over. When he did, Laura seemed surprised. "I don't think of Marty as a thief!" she said. "Marty's a terrific kid. I adore him." She went on to explain to Joe that children Marty's age don't really have a concept of stealing. "They still think that wishing something were theirs has the power to make it so."

Joe also told Laura he'd found it embarrassing to have her search Marty's pockets in front of the other parents. "What are they going to think?" Laura apologized and said she'd leave it to Joe to make sure Marty left the school's cars at school.

It's common for parents to feel responsible for their child's every action and to feel embarrassed when their child does something that's generally considered wrong.

Parents often fear that any misbehavior by their child reflects on them—they're not raising their child well enough, or their family has lax standards or bad values.

An incident like Joe's with Marty can be especially hard if it taps into an experience the parent had as a child. Joe had a painful memory of a neighbor accusing him of stealing when he was a child. Joe, who was about seven at the time, had helped himself to the neighbor's shovel one day when he wanted to dig worms from the garden. He knew he wasn't stealing, but he'd felt angry and humiliated. Some remnant of that old feeling was aroused by Laura's "search."

Even if an old button isn't being pushed, parents identify closely with their children and are sensitive to comments about their behavior. Try to be aware that most providers and teachers don't automatically assume you're doing something wrong as a parent if your child misbehaves. Your provider is more apt to view your child's behavior as a normal part of growing up.

Parents also worry that a child's early behavior may predict later behavior. If a child takes what he wants, his parents may think they have a budding kleptomaniac on their hands. But the magical thinking young children do makes it perfectly sensible to them to take what they want. Laura pointed out to Joe that three-year-old Marty wouldn't think of taking a car as stealing. A young child simply assumes that if he wants something, it's all right to take it. Young children are egocentric. Their brains have not yet developed to a point where they can see the world from multiple perspectives; they do not differentiate between what they want and what they can or cannot have. Once he understood this, Joe didn't have to rationalize Marty's behavior as forgetting. His behavior made sense in the world of a three-year-old, and Joe could collaborate with Laura in teaching Marty without feeling embarrassed or judged.

Saucy Sally

At five years old, Sally was attending her last year of preschool before starting kindergarten in the fall. Sally adored her thirteen-year-old sister and mimicked her constantly. One day when her mom was picking her up from preschool, she witnessed something she thought was very cute and funny.

The teacher had asked Sally to put away the dress-up clothes she'd been playing with before she left. Sally put one hand on her out-thrust hip, looked at her teacher, rolled her eyes, and said. "Whatever!" Her mom laughed. "You sound just like your big sister," she said. She noticed, however, that Sally's teacher hadn't laughed. She just waited until Sally started putting away the doll clothes, when she said, "Thank you."

While Sally completed her task, the teacher took Corrine aside and told her it wasn't a good idea to laugh at that kind of behavior. It would reinforce Sally's disrespectful behavior. Although it might be okay in certain situations, there were a lot of places in Sally's life where that kind of behavior was not going to be appreciated.

Corrine was startled, and then felt ashamed and

annoyed at the same time. "Yeah, well, we have a sense of humor at our house."

"I'm sorry," the teacher replied. "I didn't mean to say that you're doing something wrong. I think a lot of the things kids do are hilarious, but I have to be careful about the kind of classroom manners I'm teaching them."

Children may experience different behavioral expectations in different settings. Sally's family liked informality, and the parents encouraged a certain amount of rebellion in their children. As long as the rebellion wasn't against rules they felt were serious and important, they enjoyed it and thought it was funny.

After thinking awhile about the teacher's comment, however, Corrine began to understand how Sally's taunt might have felt disrespectful to the teacher. The next time Sally did something similar, Corrine said to her, "I understand that you want to be like your big sister, and Daddy and I do think it's pretty funny sometimes. But it's not okay to do something like that at child care." Children can learn that there are ways to behave at Grandma's house, ways to behave at child care, ways to behave in a restaurant, and so on. It's useful for them to learn behaviors that are appropriate in various settings.

Rosario's Coat

Paula, who operated a child care out of her home, had one assistant and took care of eleven children. For some time, she'd been struggling with three-year-old Rosario about putting on his own coat for outings, and she was very frustrated. Rosario would argue with her and would always say, "No, you do it." Paula had three younger children who weren't old enough to manage putting their own coats on, but Rosario was old enough. If he would just do it himself, going places would be a lot easier.

One chilly autumn afternoon Paula told the children it was time to get their coats on so they could play in the backyard awhile. The children all loved playing in the sandbox and on the swing set. Sure enough, when she asked Rosario to put on his coat, he said, "You do it." Paula dug in her heels, and they argued. Finally, Paula asked her assistant to take the rest of the children out while she stayed inside cleaning up. "If you won't put on your coat," she said to Rosario, "you'll stay inside with me."

When Amanda, Rosario's grandma, came to pick him up, she found all the other children outside playing while Rosario sat long faced inside. "What's this about?" she asked. Paula explained that Rosario refused to put on his own coat, and since she didn't have time to always do that for him, Rosario had stayed inside to help her clean.

"We always put his coat on at home," Amanda said. "It's much quicker that way."

As Paula started to respond, she glanced at Rosario, who was watching them intently. She asked Amanda to come into the kitchen with her for a minute so they could talk privately. Then she explained to Amanda that she had several children younger than Rosario who couldn't put on their coats, and it ended up taking a lot of time when she had to help older children as well. In the end, it meant less playtime for all the children.

Amanda said she could understand that, but she also knew that Rosario was quick to get into power struggles. She wondered whether Paula needed to approach him differently.

As soon as Amanda pointed this out, Paula recognized that she'd been so frustrated that she'd allowed herself to get into a power struggle with a three-year-old. "Of course," she said, "You're right. I do want him to be more independent at school, but I need to find a better way to teach him." Paula and Rosario's grandmother decided they would both start teaching him how to put on his coat, one step at a time, and little by little they'd wean him from this piece of dependence.

Teachers and providers are apt to look at everything they do with children during the day from a developmental or educational perspective. They tend to consider learning to put on outdoor clothing in the same way a primary school teacher might consider learning to write or read. A parent may view helping a child put on his coat as a sign of love and comfort for the child, whereas the teacher focuses on teaching the child independence, as well as on being efficient as she takes care of multiple children.

Differences in perspective can be reconciled. In the last example, Paula and Amanda both understood each other's perspectives better as they talked, and they were able to find a way in which they could cooperate in teaching Rosario a skill he needed to learn.

It's important to remember that providers and teachers are also humans, and they make mistakes just like parents do. Teachers and providers can get caught in power struggles and not recognize what has happened. This doesn't mean they are bad teachers or providers. It may simply mean that they got overwhelmed or one of their buttons got pushed. If this should happen to you, it's important that you speak up and point out your concern. It's equally important to remain respectful and understanding. You should be able to expect that the teacher or provider will be open to your concerns and to expect that conflicts generally can be solved.

• • •

Points to Remember and Discuss

- Both parents and providers have to face common children's stage-related skills and behaviors—difficulty separating, ownership issues, and autonomy issues—that can be challenging.

- Because of the demands that accompany dealing with a group of children, providers have a different perspective on developmentally related challenges than parents do.

- Providers often are able to shed light on the developmental needs of children and to help parents understand how normal challenging behavior usually is.

- Through regular and open communication with your provider about these needs and challenges, you can come up with solutions that support your child in learning new behaviors.

A Good Fit

Chapter 9
When Nothing Seems to Work

No matter how cautious you are or how much effort you put into finding the best child care fit for your child and your family, problems may crop up. As we've seen in previous chapters, parents and providers have to work at their partnership in caring for a child. Sometimes you may find yourself wondering if you've chosen the wrong place. Joe wondered for a time after Laura took the Matchbox cars out of Marty's pockets. Rachel wondered if she'd chosen a place so focused on Christian holidays that her Jewish child could never fit in. Fatuma and Yusuf wondered if Naja's provider was so lax about television and so disrespectful of their wishes that they'd need to find a new place.

In each of these cases, the parents were able to work out some resolution with the provider. Challenges often crop up in child care settings, but usually they can be solved. It requires that you keep an open mind and take some initiative in talking with your provider and thinking about solutions. But sometimes, nothing seems to work.

Calling It Quits

Many things can cause parents to think about moving their child to a new place, but, no matter what the reason is, it should be done with caution and after careful consideration. Katya thought about moving her son when she thought the teacher didn't greet him with the same enthusiasm with which she greeted the other children. It turned out the provider was purposely keeping a low profile with Alex because when she'd greeted him enthusiastically the first day, he quickly pulled back from her. It was her sense that Alex didn't like rushing into things and needed time to feel comfortable with her. Katya came to realize that it was the provider's job to figure out the dance with Alex at child care, and she could count on her to do this.

Naomi thought about pulling her child because she thought the other families were unfriendly. Then one day another mother walked out at the same time as Naomi and they struck up a conversation. Naomi invited her over for coffee, and soon Naomi felt like part of the community.

If you feel like giving up on your child care setting, don't be hasty. Just as there are many challenges that prompt parents to think about changing, there are also many annoyances that don't justify such a move. For example, you probably don't need to worry if there are a couple of new children at your center who've been acting out and playing too rough for a while. As we've discussed, all children go through difficult transitions and phases, and a good provider knows how to help children through such periods while also supporting the other children. It's generally better for your child if you can avoid a change. Transitions are always a challenge, and children sometimes feel like they've done something wrong if they have to go to a new child care.

How can you tell the difference between a bump in the road and a pothole so big you can't climb out of it? How can you tell when it's time to call it quits? Described below are some reasons why you might want to consider withdrawing your child from a child care setting.

> If There Are Significant Health and Safety Risks

You do not, of course, want to risk your child's health and safety. But this doesn't mean you need to withdraw your child if another child in the program has a serious illness from which your child can be protected, even a condition as serious as acquired immunodeficiency syndrome (AIDS). Children in care can be protected from AIDS. As of the publication date of this book, there had been no documented case of a caregiver or any child in care contracting AIDS from a child. If, however, your child is always coming down with something because your provider regularly allows children with communicable diseases to come to child care when they're still contagious, you might consider looking for alternatives.

There may be no reason to withdraw your child if your provider takes him on adventurous outings. Trips to the zoo or to the community swimming pool can be handled safely and can be wonderful experiences for your child. If, however, your provider drives your two-year-old on outings without putting him in a car seat, that is an unacceptable risk. Perhaps you can talk with the provider about never doing that again and trust her to keep her word. Or you may decide that her showing such a profound lack of judgment makes it impossible for you to take that risk. Situations often must be judged individually.

> If You Cannot Establish a Baseline of Trust

If you really don't trust the provider to give you accurate information, it may be time to move your child. Gerry moved his child when he discovered the provider had lied to him about her son living with her. He'd liked the provider very much. Her house was always clean, she was creative and nurturing, and his daughter loved it there. But then the provider's son, who'd been convicted of making and dealing methamphetamine, was released from jail and moved back into her home.

Understandably, the provider wanted to support her son, and she believed he'd benefited from treatment and wasn't a safety risk. She was also afraid the parents wouldn't trust her son, so she hid the fact that he'd moved home. Gerry thought this was an irreparable breach of faith. If you think a provider is not trustworthy, it may be time to move your child.

You should be able to give your provider any information important to the welfare of your child without worrying that she won't keep it confidential. Similarly, you should be able to share information, ask questions, or ask for advice without feeling judged. Problems in either of these areas may be an indication that critical respect is lacking.

>If the School or Home Is Too Rigid

Sometimes a provider's rules are so rigid that compromise is impossible. Perhaps any deviation is simply unacceptable to the provider, and even when you think your son needs some kind of accommodation, she isn't open to any kind of discussion. Or you may find that when you drop by to observe, you're not allowed into the classroom or home. This is a red flag. The National Association for the Education of Young Children (NAEYC) Code of Ethical Conduct requires that parents have access to the spaces their children are in at all times.

>If Infants Aren't Protected Sufficiently from Older Children

Older children are fascinated by babies. They love to touch and talk to and hug infants. A setting that has a mixture of kindergartners, preschoolers, toddlers, and infants must keep very close tabs on child-to-child interactions. If you think your infant isn't being watched closely enough, you may want to consider changing providers. For instance, if you see a three-year-old pick up an infant who's sitting in an infant chair and carry him around the room without the provider noticing, that's cause for concern. If an infant gets knocked out of a chair by running toddlers or cuddled so hard she can hardly breathe, you may want to start looking for a new place.

Other signs that your child is at risk of injury include unmonitored play on equipment that is dangerous or meant for older children, stairs that don't have gates, and untreated injuries of any kind. Any sign that your child isn't physically safe is a definite signal that it's time to look for another setting. As always, after just one incident, you need to express your concerns and be firm in your expectations that appropriate changes will be made. According to the severity of the situation, if the provider addresses the problem and everything is going well otherwise, you may want to give that setting another chance.

>If Your Child Continues to Show Anxiety or Fails to Develop a Bond with the Provider

As you know, it's natural for a child to need some time to adjust to a new child care setting. But if the anxiety continues for several months, it's possible that a setting simply is not the right fit for your child. Another indication of a bad fit is when your child isn't forming a bond with the provider. It's natural for children over three years of age to be more interested in playing with the other children and less focused on the provider, but a younger child should eventually be consistently relaxed and comfortable in the company of the provider. If that's not the case with your child, it doesn't necessarily mean that the provider is incompetent. Some personalities simply clash, even in a relationship between a child care professional and a young child, and sometimes, despite a provider's best efforts, a genuine bond simply fails to form.

>If Your Child Just Doesn't Seem to Be Thriving

Sometimes parents find that their child always looks bored or uninvolved at child care or preschool. Perhaps he just sits expressionless and seems lethargic, even though this is not characteristic of him. You can't put your finger on anything specific, but your child simply isn't thriving. If, even though you can't figure out why, your intuition tells you your child is not stimulated or happy, you may want to check out some other settings.

On rare occasions a parent may have to move a child because an initial choice fails to work out as the parent thought it would. Perhaps the setting simply isn't a good match for a child. Sometimes parents finally decide that moving their child is the best answer.

Moving Tiffany

We met Joan at the beginning of this book. She and her husband, Ron, had had Tiffany in Terry's family child care for three years. There'd been a few problems to work out early on in the relationship, but they now had a wonderful understanding with Terry. She was wise and knowledgeable about children and had helped Joan and Ron through Tiffany's toilet training and her nothing but "No" phase. Terry had helped them teach Tiffany to use her words instead of her fists when she was angry. Tiffany went to the library every week with Terry and the other children in the child care, and she was starting to recognize a few printed words. She had good friends in Terry's child care and loved going there. So when a seemingly unsolvable problem arose, Joan and Ron were torn about what to do.

Terry's mother had been diagnosed with Alzheimer's disease, and she'd moved in with Terry not long after the diagnosis. She was sometimes a bit confused but not in a way that affected the children. She was instead a loving, caring grandmother to them. As time went on, however, her condition worsened, and Joan and Ron could see that stress was taking its toll on Terry. She was tired a lot and looked overwhelmed. They didn't want to intrude on her personal life, but they also worried about whether she had the stamina to care for both her mother and the children. They finally decided to talk to her about it. They approached her gingerly. "We sometimes wonder if it's getting to be too much," Joan said.

"I can handle this," Terry replied firmly. "Don't worry about me. I may look tired, but I'm arranging for my brother to care for Mom every Friday and Saturday, and that will give me a chance to catch up on things around here and get some downtime."

Joan and Ron were relieved to hear Terry's answer. They didn't want to move Tiffany, and by now they really cared about Terry as well, so it was great to know she'd be getting the help she needed.

Then one day, Tiffany came home with an alarming story. "Grandma Millie got lost today," she reported. They'd gone to the park, and Terry's mother loved going along. But on this day, she'd wandered off and Terry had to hurry the children home and then call the police to find her. "The policeman brought Grandma Millie home," Tiffany said.

Joan and Ron looked at each other. "I'm so glad they found her, honey," Joan said. That night they discussed whether Grandma Millie was presenting a safety issue at child care. Were her needs becoming so great that Terry could get distracted from taking care of the children?

Could she keep her eyes on the children and her mother at the same time?

"She'd never put the kids' safety at risk," Joan said. "You know that, Ron." Both of them had a great deal of trust in Terry. They talked with Terry again, and again she was adamant about having everything under control. It was an aberration, she said; her mother wasn't really that bad yet. She'd been unusually stressed and that had temporarily made her more confused. Terry was putting fail-safe systems in place, but they could rest assured that the children's safety would always come first with her. She never, for instance, would have considered leaving the children in the park to go look for her mother.

"We know that," Ron said.

But the concern stayed with them. The following Friday, Tiffany came home and told them about a fire in the kitchen. Grandma Millie had taken a pot off the stove and left the burner on. When Josh set his drawing on the stove, it went up in flames. They met with Terry on Saturday. "This is excruciating," Joan told her, "but we've decided to put Tiffany in the Riverside School for Young Children. Tiffany loves it here. We love it here. And we know you're in a really hard place. But we think there are safety risks now."

Terry ultimately came to terms with what her mother needed and found an Alzheimer's unit for her, but not before Ron and Joan moved Tiffany. They felt they had no choice but to move their daughter. It's not always obvious when a safety risk becomes unacceptable. Joan and Ron may have put off the move longer than they should have because they had such a good history with Terry. They also didn't want to hurt Tiffany's feelings. If you're worried about safety, you've spoken with the provider, and you're still not satisfied that your child is safe, you really have no choice. Your child's safety comes first.

A Matter of Temperament

Cameo was a lively, outgoing child, the kind who went after whatever she wanted. She climbed on beds and dressers and kitchen cabinets. She chased the cat into the front yard, and painted a village on her bedroom wall. She quickly became the center of attention in any room, and she loved adult attention.

Her parents were entirely taken with the program at the Cascade Creek Preschool. Although they'd never heard of a Reggio Emilia program, they fell in love with it immediately. It seemed perfectly suited for Cameo. The children were all talking and laughing and moving around. There were no hushed voices. Artwork hung everywhere, and growing things sprouted from window boxes and from pots hung from the ceiling and from inside the loft house in the corner. It was much more full of life than anything either of her parents had had when they were Cameo's age. It was love at first sight. And the artist-in-residence program sealed the deal for Darlene. "We're home," she said.

It turned out to be perfect for Cameo. It took her about two days to make the transition. She was soon running full speed ahead each morning when her dad dropped her off. And, as she went along playing, she seemed to be learning everything she needed for kindergarten. She could read the whole alphabet and a few words, and she knew her numbers to twenty. The family couldn't have been happier.

When Eddie was born, Darlene and Paul already knew where they'd be sending him. How nice, they thought, not to have to go through a big search again. They kept Eddie in a family child care until he was two-and-a-half, and then moved him to Cascade Creek. It felt wonderful to be back in those lively rooms, and the director was delighted to see them again.

But Eddie didn't thrive. His parents knew transitions were difficult for him, so they'd expected it would take some time for him to get used to the new place. He was very sensitive. As an infant, he'd startled much more easily than Cameo had. He didn't sleep through loud noises the way she did, and he fussed about little things like the seams in his socks. He was quite different from Cameo in a lot of ways. He was quiet and when he came into a room, he held back.

Paul and Darlene were both pretty extroverted, and they wanted Eddie to learn how to make friends. They wanted him to be a go-getter, to be ready to take on the world when he grew up. This preschool, they thought, was exactly the right step for him.

Six months after Eddie started Cascade Creek, he was still clinging tightly to Darlene when she dropped him off. Darlene felt exasperated, but she also felt sad and worried. His teacher told Darlene that Eddie didn't seem at ease there. He needed comforting repeatedly during the day, and he often stayed on the sidelines. No matter how many things she tried, she couldn't seem to engage Eddie in the groups of children for very long. He seemed to be overwhelmed by the noise and commotion. She finally suggested to Darlene that Cascade Creek might not be the right place for Eddie.

Darlene cried about it. "I love this place," she said. "I love the other families here. This is my place."

"I know," answered the teacher. "That's exactly it. This is your place. It was perfect for Cameo and we love your involvement. But I'm not sure it's Eddie's place."

The teacher talked with Darlene about temperamental differences. She wondered aloud if Eddie might not do better in a smaller place with fewer children, if he'd do better with a little less noise and commotion and a little more structure.

It can be hard to accept that your child is very different from you or from a sibling who's been particularly delightful. As parents, we often identify closely with our children, and it can be as hard for us to separate from them as it is for them to separate from us. But it's important that we allow our children to be who they are, that we revisit forcing them into our picture of who we want them to be. Darlene was not unusual in her yearning for Eddie to be more like her and her husband and to respond to the world like his sister Cameo. It was hard for her to hear what the teacher had to say.

She went home and talked it over with Paul, who was also disappointed. But the bottom line was that they loved Eddie and wanted what was best for him. Luckily

Eddie had a teacher who was attuned to his needs and parents who were able to hear that he needed something different. They enrolled him in a much smaller neighborhood preschool with a structured program, and ultimately both Darlene and Paul were happy about it. Eddie was able to grow and bloom in his new setting. Because transitions were hard for him, it took awhile before he could quit hanging on to Darlene at drop-off time, but within a month he was at ease and waving good-bye quite happily.

• • •

Points to Remember and Discuss

You should be cautious in making the decision to remove your child from a child care setting. Transitions are generally challenging for children, so you should work with the provider and do everything you can to find solutions. There are times, however, when nothing more can be done and it's time to move. It may be time to call it quits if

- there are significant health and safety risks,
- you cannot establish a baseline of trust,
- the school or home is too rigid,
- the interaction between older children and infants is insufficiently protected,
- your child continues to show anxiety for several months,
- your child fails to develop a bond with the provider,
- your child just doesn't seem to be thriving.

Chapter 10
Weighing the Pros and Cons

Whether you're making the difficult decision to move your child from a setting that isn't working, moving to a new town or neighborhood, or looking for child care for the first time, a lot of effort goes into choosing the right setting for your child.

What to Consider When You're Choosing

Typically, when parents are looking for child care, their first considerations are practical: location, hours, and cost. This makes sense. You certainly don't want your life to be more difficult than it has to be. But other considerations may override convenience.

First, of course, is the provider herself or himself. You'll want to weigh whether she seems warm and nurturing enough. Whether he's firm enough. Whether she's fair enough. Whether he's knowledgeable enough. Parents are right to give providers serious consideration. Child care or preschool isn't a service you're purchasing. What you're doing is inviting another important person or group of persons into your life and into your child's life.

You'll want to know whether those persons have the skills and temperament to work well with your child. You'll also want to know that they have enough flexibility and enough respect for parents to form a good working relationship with them.

You'll also want to think about the other issues considered in this book. Look at the policies of the setting and consider whether they fit with the needs of your family. Look into the setting's values and decide whether they're similar enough to yours that you can live with them. If you find profound differences in values or a set of policies for which you cannot comfortably find compromises, you may need to keep looking.

Even if you like the provider and are comfortable with the policies and values, you'll also want to know that the setting itself is safe and of good quality. To help you determine the quality of a program, you can check to see if a setting you're considering is licensed. Many states have licensing for preschools and family child care. Although licensing may indicate only that minimum standards are being met, it can still be a good place to start assessing quality. Accreditation by the National Association for the Education of Young Children (NAEYC) provides another benchmark. A program's accreditation can be checked on the NAEYC Web site. The Web site also has a brochure that contains a checklist of quality indicators for infants, for toddlers, and for preschoolers. For a good overview of what to do and what to look for, see the appendix, "Choosing Quality Child Care," at the end of this book.

As you're choosing a new setting for your child, or finding one for the first time, you can go by your gut reaction, of course. That's important. But it's also important to think carefully about the setting and whether it's a good fit for your child. Described below are some pitfalls parents can fall into when choosing child care settings.

>Choosing What's a Good Fit for You More Than for Your Child

It's important to differentiate your desires from your child's needs and nature. It's very common to walk into a preschool or child care and think, "Oh, I would have so much fun here if I were a child. This is perfect." But your child is not you. Make sure you stop to consider whether it fits his or her personality.

As we saw in the last chapter, Eddie's parents loved places that were highly creative, places where everyone was doing their own thing and it was noisy and fluid and exciting. Their first child fit into such a setting perfectly. But not Eddie. He was a child who thrived on structure and known expectations and who felt lost in an environment so full of commotion. His parents had been so excited by the program, so pleased with it, that they hadn't given themselves the time or space to think about whether it was the right place for a child with Eddie's personality.

Parents will sometimes choose a setting because it focuses on something one of them has a passion for—music, for instance. Or they might choose a program that focuses on another special niche such as the outdoors or athletics. It's human nature to want to encourage your child in exploring the things that fascinate you. But it's just as important to remain aware of his or her interests. A program that's based on a music curriculum may have too narrow a focus for your child if music isn't her thing. The point is to find a program that fits your child's style.

> Choosing by Reputation

Parents often find child care or preschools through word of mouth. It can feel reassuring to put your child in a program that's popular with your friends. But the program that's right for your friends' children isn't necessarily the best one for your child. Programs tend to get reputations; sometimes they're deserved and sometimes they're not. Sometimes they get a reputation for being good simply because they're hard to get into. It's worth investigating a number of places. An unknown small program or a family child care down the street may be a better fit for your child. Be open to checking a variety of options, and don't worry if other people don't agree with your choice. You know your child best.

> Choosing for the Future instead of for Now

Parents sometimes feel pressure to pick a school that's going to get their child into a certain private elementary school, or they feel they ought to put their child in a skill-and-drill kind of program so he can pass the test required to get into a certain school. Be cautious here: The school that best prepares kids for the future is a school that gives them developmentally appropriate experiences in the present. You cannot predict what the world will look like for your child in five or ten years; the most important thing you can give her is a positive growing experience now.

Conclusion

The vast majority of parents in today's society are parents who work outside the home. Some parents do so reluctantly and feel guilty about leaving their young children in the care of others. Some parents do so confidently, believing the experience is broadening for their children. The many parents who are somewhere in between feel ambivalent about the benefits, the loss, the potential growth, the challenges. Whatever your attitude may be, it's a good bet that choosing a child care and then monitoring and evaluating your child's ongoing experience in the setting you've chosen seems like a daunting task.

There are many wonderful child care settings and programs and many types from which to choose. No matter which kind of setting you choose, remember that one of the most important things you can do to make it a successful experience is to form and maintain a collaborative partnership with your provider.

The parent/provider relationship has been likened to a marriage without the vows. It's a relationship you have to work at. It requires that you be honest, direct, and understanding, that you hold reasonable expectations, and that you be open to listening and compromise. It's a relationship in which you should expect trustworthiness, confidentiality, and mutual respect. It's a relationship that requires thoughtful exploration of your child's developmental needs and learning style and consideration of what you can do to stimulate and support his physical, cognitive, and emotional development and also meet his creative, educational, and social needs. Above all, it's a relationship that's all about your child—giving him the best possible experience, giving her plenty of support and guidance, giving them the security that will allow them to grow.

• • •

Points to Remember and Discuss

- Your goal in choosing a new setting—whether you're moving your child or choosing for the first time—is to find a preschool, home, or center in which your child makes friends, explores, experiments with new things, and feels safe and happy.

- You need to keep in mind practical considerations such as hours, distance, and costs.

- You also need to keep in mind the less concrete considerations: the policies, the values, and the educational principles that are reflected in the program.

- You need to be wary of choosing more for what you like than for meeting your child's unique needs or choosing based on reputation alone or choosing in response to passing trends.

- Most important of all are the qualifications, skills, and attitude of the provider and her willingness to build with you a working relationship with the goal of doing what's best for your child.

Appendix
Choosing Quality Child Care

Because profound growth and change occur during the first five years of a child's life, the child care experience you choose can play a significant role in your child's physical, social, emotional, and cognitive development. The child care field has responded to increased awareness of the importance of early learning and development by offering families a variety of quality care options.

Setting Goals That Meet Your Childs Needs

As you go about choosing child care, keep in mind the goals and values that are uniquely important to your family. Remember that what may be an ideal care arrangement for a neighbor or a coworker may not be what works well for your child or family. If it's important to you that siblings who need care have plenty of time together, you'll probably want to look for a licensed home or a center where children are in mixed-age groups. If, on the other hand, you believe your child would benefit from a larger group experience with the opportunity to interact with a variety of children and adults, you might want to look at child care centers.

Just as there are many different parenting styles, quality child care comes in many different models. It's important that you choose a model and setting that both supports your family values and goals and meets the quality standards you decide are essential for your child. Rates vary by type of program, qualifications of staff, adult-child ratios, and demographics, and better programs often cost more. If a program you like is priced outside your budget, look into funding assistance options such as the child care tax credit and dependent-care flex spending accounts.

Before choosing a child care setting, take the time to carefully consider your answers to these questions:

- What is my child like? What personality traits have emerged?
- What are my child's special needs now? What possible future needs might my child have?
- What are my child's interests? Have any special skills become apparent?
- What are my family's practical needs—schedule, budget, and so on?
- What values and traditions—religious and cultural ones, for instance—are important to my family?
- What goals do I have for my child? Do I want my child to:

    >learn how to play well with others?

>be more independent and confident?

>be prepared for school?

>have a fun, safe experience?

Child Care Options

Although there are a variety of child care models—some based on a specific philosophy or approach, such as Montessori or Reggio, and others with a religious or cultural focus—there are three basic settings in which child care is delivered.

- In-Home Care. The caregiver, who may be a family member, a friend, or a professional provider, comes into your home.
- Family Child Care. The caregiver provides care for your child and other children, usually of various ages, in his or her home. Family child care providers should be licensed or registered by your state or county agency.
- School-Based or Independent Child Care Centers. Your child is cared for by a staff—usually one trained in early childhood education—in a regulated setting that often has educationally designed play areas and a schedule of programmed activities for children grouped by age.

To find out about programs available in your area, look up your regional Child Care Resource and Referral Agency. Because they vary from state to state, you'll need to ask your local agency what the licensing requirements and standards are for your state. You can also ask your agency if any violations have been reported for centers or homes on your list of prospective settings.

Visiting Child Care Settings

Selecting the type of child care that will work best for your family may take some time. It's important that you visit each child care setting you're considering (seeing a minimum of three is recommended) and, if possible, that you revisit the settings you liked the first time around. While visiting, pay attention to the interactions of the children with each other and with the provider. For a significant portion of any given day, the atmosphere should be pleasant, the children should be engaged in stimulating activities, and the provider should be interacting with or available to the children.

When children are involved, conflicts are inevitable. If a conflict arises while you're visiting, you'll have a wonderful opportunity to see whether the provider responds in a caring and developmentally appropriate way and is sensitive to the children's emotional needs. As they grow and develop, children experience anger and sadness along with all the joys and happiness of childhood. They need the support of knowledgeable, caring adults as they learn to identify and deal with their emotions effectively. In quality child care settings, children receive a lot of adult attention and assistance in learning how to identify and manage their emotions as they participate in activities and interact with other children and adults.

As part of each visit, you'll want to ask the provider

or director about her setting's policies and practices. Common policy issues and topics to ask about include injuries and illness, emergencies and disasters, being late, holidays and vacations, bringing toys and other personal belongings from home, television watching, behavior challenges and discipline, toilet training, parent communication and conferences, safety and security, and meals and nutrition. Most homes and centers should have written-down policies. Ask for a copy. If topics you need to know about aren't covered, ask the provider about them and add that information to your copy for future reference.

Quality Child Care Environments

Each child care setting you visit will be different, and the facilities of child care centers will be very different from home care settings. But in any setting, there are general benchmarks of quality care to look for. During a reasonable length of time in a child care setting, you should see these indicators of quality:

1. Children are given the opportunity to engage in large-motor activities, including
- building, sorting, and stacking with a variety of materials such as large blocks;
- organized active small group games and exercises;
- free time to run, jump, and climb both outside and in, in groups and individually.

2. Social interaction is facilitated both formally in small

group activities and informally in play with another child or with several other children.

3. Children are given opportunities to develop emerging literacy, math, science, and artistic skills through age-appropriate play and manipulation of materials of a variety of sizes, shapes, and colors:
- interesting objects to count and sort
- blocks and puzzles for learning spatial relationships
- markers, crayons, and pencils for writing and drawing
- books to read and to have read to them
- building materials that promote problem solving and emerging math skills
- games that involve matching, sequencing, and classification, which are the cornerstones for math and reading

4. Children's creativity is encouraged through opportunities to engage in painting, drawing, singing, dancing, storytelling, and playing with puppets, dolls, and toy animals.

5. The environment is clean and safe for all the children because
- children are supervised at all times by an adult (a minimum adult-to-child ratio of one to four for infants and one to ten for preschool ages is recommended);
- the toys are appropriate for the age of the children and are in good condition;
- there are no safety hazards such as stairs without proper railings, exposed wiring, uncovered outlets,

access to tools or medicine, or dangerous pets;

- infants and toddlers are protected from the rough play of older children;
- the atmosphere is pleasant and inviting to children and their families;
- the setting is usually calm and often is filled with the happy sounds of children playing;
- the provider speaks to the children respectfully and maintains discipline without shouting or threatening;
- the children have a secure place where they can keep their personal belongings.

Accreditation

Accreditation is the status given to early childhood programs that have completed an extensive evaluation process based on state and national standards for quality care. To become accredited, a program must participate in an extensive self-study that includes parent evaluation and observation by a trained validation expert. Both child care centers and family child programs may be accredited. Accreditation, however, is not a guarantee of quality. It is a voluntary system to set professional standards and to help families identify high-quality programs. It is simply one tool for helping families evaluate and choose child care.

Provider Credentials

The most important component of quality child care is the relationship your child has with the care provider.

Children who have nurturing, responsive, and stable relationships with caring adults generally grow up to be healthier and more competent than children who don't. Research has shown that relationships are a key component to healthy brain development. While observing a child care setting, be sure to look for indications of the relationships the provider has with individual children as well as her rapport with the group. Some questions you may want to ask the provider include the following:

- What experience do you have in working with children, especially children who have characteristics similar to my child's?

- What is your educational experience? The educational requirements for child care providers vary from state to state. Provider credentials can include the completion of a few specific courses, a two-year or four-year college degree in early childhood development, a child development associate degree, a teaching degree, or even a master's degree. Regardless of the type of education a provider has, she or he should be licensed or certified. Studies have shown that one of the best predictors of quality child care is the amount of ongoing training and education the provider receives.

- [if the child care setting is a center] Who are all the people who would be caring for my child and what are their qualifications?

- How long might my child be with a particular provider or teacher? [In other words, what are the teacher turnover rates and, if the children transition to other providers or teachers as they age, how is that transition conducted?]

- What is your philosophy on the care and education of children and what methods do you use? [In other words, how well does the provider's viewpoint fit your family's values and goals?]

The Parent/Provider Relationship

As stressed in this and the other books in this series, the best child care arrangement is one in which the parents and provider work together to provide the guidance, nurturing, and experiences that foster the child's growth and development. A professional child care provider recognizes the parent as the most important influence on the child's development. Good parenting includes seeking information about your child's behavior, interests, skills, and development from knowledgeable resources such as a professional provider. The best way to ensure quality child care is to maintain daily, meaningful communication with your chosen child care provider and to become actively involved in parent activities. Whether you choose a family child care, a child care center, or a professional to care for your child in your home, a quality child care experience should promote your child's health, growth, and education in a fun and safe setting.

Resources for Finding Quality Child Care

www.childcareaware.org (800-424-2246)
A national organization to assist families with child care. This site includes a tool to search for family and center child care in your area. Offered in both English and Spanish.

www.naeyc.org
The National Association for the Education of Young Children. This site has information on accreditation for families as well as a search function for accredited child care centers and kindergartens in your area.

www.nafcc.org
The National Association for Family Child Care. This site has a search function for accredited family child care in your area.

About the Author

Julie Powers has worked as a teacher, administrator, and college educator in early childhood education and has presented workshops on parent and provider relationships at conferences throughout the United States. She holds a master's degree from Pacific Oaks College, with specialization in both early childhood education and parent/community work. She is the author of *Parent-Friendly Early Learning: Tips and Strategies for Working Well with Families,* and has had several articles published in *Child Care Information Exchange*. She is also a parent, whose child was in child care. She lives in Placerville, Colorado.

For over thirty years, Redleaf Press has been a leading publisher of exceptional professional resources for the early childhood field. Redleaf Guides for Parents offer parents field-tested, cutting-edge thinking about creating positive partnerships with the adults who care for their children.